DARK PSYCHOLOGY

Learn How to Read Facial Expressions and Body Language

(Find Out the Secrets of Emotional Intelligence)

Lula Bennett

Published by Sharon Lohan

© **Lula Bennett**

All Rights Reserved

Dark Psychology: Learn How to Read Facial Expressions and Body Language (Find Out the Secrets of Emotional Intelligence)

ISBN 978-1-990334-54-2

All rights reserved. No part of this guide may be reproduced in any form without permission in writing from the publisher except in the case of brief quotations embodied in critical articles or reviews.

Legal & Disclaimer

The information contained in this book is not designed to replace or take the place of any form of medicine or professional medical advice. The information in this book has been provided for educational and entertainment purposes only.

The information contained in this book has been compiled from sources deemed reliable, and it is accurate to the best of the Author's knowledge; however, the Author cannot guarantee its accuracy and validity and cannot be held liable for any errors or omissions. Changes are periodically made to this book. You must consult your doctor or get professional medical advice before using any of the suggested remedies, techniques, or information in this book.

Upon using the information contained in this book, you agree to hold harmless the Author from and against any damages, costs, and expenses, including any legal fees potentially resulting from the application of any of the information provided by this guide. This disclaimer applies to any damages or injury caused by the use and application, whether directly or indirectly, of any advice or information presented, whether for breach of contract, tort, negligence, personal injury, criminal intent, or under any other cause of action.

You agree to accept all risks of using the information presented inside this book. You need to consult a professional medical practitioner in order to ensure you are both able and healthy enough to participate in this program.

Table of Contents

INTRODUCTION 1

CHAPTER 1: THE ART OF PERSUASION NLP 5

CHAPTER 2: HOW TO USE NEURO-LINGUISTIC PROGRAMMING (NLP) 17

CHAPTER 3: MANIPULATION 29

CHAPTER 4: THE DARK TRIAD 41

CHAPTER 5: WHAT IS NEURO-LINGUISTICS? 49

CHAPTER 6: UNDERSTANDING PSYCHOPATHS 63

CHAPTER 7: SAFEGUARDING YOURSELF FROM DARK PSYCHOLOGISTS 70

CHAPTER 8: MANIPULATION 88

CHAPTER 9: THE ART OF PERSUASION 98

CHAPTER 10: USING NEURO-LINGUISTIC PROGRAMMING TO "MANIPULATE" THE MIND 112

CHAPTER 11: SNEAKY WAYS OF COVERT HYPNOSIS 120

CHAPTER 12: BRAINWASHING 132

CHAPTER 13: BRAINWASHING AND OTHER MIND CONTROL TACTICS 156

CHAPTER 14: LEARN HOW TO USE MANIPULATION TO YOUR ADVANTAGE 174

CHAPTER 15: LEARN THE BASICS OF MANIPULATION .... ERROR! BOOKMARK NOT DEFINED.

CHAPTER 16: COVERT EMOTIONAL MANIPULATION TECHNIQUES .... ERROR! BOOKMARK NOT DEFINED.

CONCLUSION 192

Introduction

With the understanding of what dark psychology is, you may be second-guessing your reasoning for delving into this dark world in the first place. Perhaps you prefer to behave in ways that are more ethically acceptable, or you feel guilty at the mere thought of influencing someone to do something that they very clearly seem to have no interest in. However, even if you do not intend to use dark psychology, you will still see several benefits to continuing to read.

Perhaps the most important reason to understand dark psychology is that through understanding it, you are better able to defend yourself in the instance that someone chooses to use dark psychology against you. You will understand what makes someone an easy victim, and you will recognize the signs and behaviors of manipulation or mind control. Through knowing how these various types of influence are used upon people, you will better recognize them.

Most of these techniques rely on the other person being unaware of their use in the first place-they require secrecy to operate as successfully as possible. That secrecy allows them to remain largely unnoticed, enabling the manipulation, coercion, persuasion, or other influence to appear to be of the individual's own volition.

When the victim cannot see the strings that the manipulator is pulling, the victim will not suspect the manipulation, making them far more susceptible. Beyond simply protecting yourself, however, there are several different ways that dark psychology can be wielded to be beneficial to everyone involved.

For example, you can utilize persuasion methods to perform better in business fields or sales jobs. Because you will know exactly how to persuade others, you will be able to identify what another person needs or wants to meet their own needs better while still managing to close the sale.

You may find that your numbers increase, and you are making sure to ensure that everyone around you is satisfied.

Perhaps you are in law or politics, and you need people to trust what you are saying and believe your arguments. You can do that by utilizing various principles of dark psychology, such as dark persuasion. Maybe you want to be a more effective parent, which would also utilize techniques like dark persuasion to convince a child that they are behaving in a certain way because they do, want to do so, rather than because their parents told them to.

Maybe you simply want to watch the world burn—if this is the case. Please recognize that this book is not meant to encourage or condone harmful behaviors. This book will provide you with all of the tools you will need to understand dark psychology. Ultimately, what you choose to do with that knowledge falls upon your shoulders. While this book encourages the use of dark psychology in ways that are beneficial for everyone involved, there is ultimately no way to stop you from engaging in those negative behaviors if that is what you plan to do.

Chapter 1: The Art Of Persuasion Nlp

Perhaps you were considering being hypnotized yourself and you wanted to know more about the process. Or, maybe you have always considered a career in psychology, in particular, hypnotherapy.

Many people wonder if hypnosis can be used to persuade people – to win arguments, negotiate purchases, and sell people things, and so on. The truth is that hypnosis truly is meant to be a therapy. That is, the field of hypnosis originated with psychologists whose goal was to help people change undesirable attitudes, fears, and behaviors. With hypnotherapy, a therapist can delve deep into a person's subconscious and reprogram how that person thinks and reacts in their waking state.

Yet there are other ways to use the subconscious.

Hypnotherapy uses several different techniques. Among these are the ideas of mirroring and leading, strategies that are part of another area of psychological study called neuro-linguistic programming, or NLP, as it is commonly called. NLP is a method of changing how we communicate with others to create more favorable outcomes for yourself and those you communicate with. That is if you understand NLP you better understand how people think and behave, and you better understand how to have productive interactions with people – interactions that accomplish goals, both yours and theirs.

We will talk briefly about NLP, teaching you a few concepts that you can use in your everyday life to have more beneficial interactions with other people. You can also use these tips if you go into hypnosis practice to build a better rapport with your subjects and to best help them achieve their goals.

NLP is a way of reading body language and mood and using this information to lead the other person where you want them to go. When you properly implement NLP, you can communicate better with your partner, be a better parent, work better with your colleagues, communicate more effectively with your boss, and more. When you learn NLP, you learn to know yourself better, to read what other people are thinking, and to have a direct impact on the world.

Psychologists and laypeople have used the practice of NLP for decades. Somewhat similar to hypnosis, NLP is both an art and a science, an idea that is founded on sound observation and research, yet a skill which is developed through practice and mindfulness. Put simply, NLP is a type of subconscious programming (just like hypnosis!); it's something that we all exhibit every day. For example, if someone says something that upsets you, you may subconsciously tighten your jaw and your body muscles, staying very still as you process the information. This is a subconscious response, part of our fight or flight tendencies, which first tell your body to freeze as you access a situation.

Many therapists use NLP techniques in counseling their clients, as NLP can be a very effective way to manage phobias and anxiety. NLP counseling can also help people who have had a difficult past (perhaps with abuse or trauma) to move on and learn to manage their memories. NLP has been used by dating coaches to help instill confidence in their clients and by marketing professionals to better reach their target markets. NLP can also be used on one's self in a very simple way but with profound outcomes. Let's look at a few of the most fundamental NLP concepts, and how you can use this subconscious programming to benefit you and others in everyday life.

NLP has been used in alternative medicine to treat illnesses like Parkinson's disease. It has also been used in psychotherapy, advertisement, sales, management, coaching, teaching, team building, and public speaking. Yes, each one of these categories is a form of manipulation to some degree. You can't go to a class, the grocery store, or even a restaurant without being subject to some form of manipulation. No matter where you are you can't escape it. It's present in advertisement posters, the tactic of that business sales clerk that stops you at the mall, the product placement in the movie you're watching, and everywhere else. However, instead of being afraid of this knowledge, you can use it to your advantage and redirect that manipulation as the wielder.

But some skilled individuals can harness this power to give them an unbeatable advantage. The techniques are best used in a one-on-one or small group environment. The fewer people involved, the easier it is to read and apply NLP methods.

NLP is a complex subject and is often taught over years. That's because it takes practice to learn the range of reactions people can express. But the promise of learning people's inner secrets makes this technique especially attractive to con artists and law enforcement.

A skilled NLP user can determine:

Which side of the brain their subject uses?

People fall along a spectrum between creative and analytical. New science shows that brain function is distributed across the brain. But it is still helpful to think of people through this lens.

Word choice, sentence structure, and associations all reveal details about the person that uses them. Left-brained people often use words that elicit emotions or experiences. Right-brained people like to include things outside their experience or expertise.

Which sense is most important to them?

We have more than the five senses (sight, sound, taste, touch, and smell) most people know about. We also have a sense of order, balance, morality, and a host of others, and each of us has one or two that are more important than the rest.

How their brain stores information.

Our brains are the most complex computers we have ever come across. They store and process billions of bits of information a second. Each one functions a little differently. One of the biggest areas of divergence is in how people store information.

Some individuals have a memory like a sponge, soaking up everything near them. Others are more like a filter that catches big chunks and allows everything to pass through. NLP techniques help people discern the difference and to what degree.

Over time, NLP users get better at keeping track of information. With enough time, users can improve their information tracking abilities to near-genius levels. This gives us an advantage over anyone who isn't as experienced or naturally gifted.

When they are lying or making things up.

People perform specific behaviors when they make things up called "tells." NLP users like me can pick up on these tells and be able to call out the liar as they lie. Some people are better than others at lying but everyone has at least one tell.

Skilled liars understand that for someone else to believe their lie, so must they. So they convince themselves of it first. They often don't display all the signs of dishonesty because they truly believe the lie as they tell it.

Practice can help people fall for their lie but the process demands a selective memory. This feature is more reliably detected than the oft-cited slight downward glance. It also proves to be a more consistent indicator of ingrained deception than awkward looks. Power imbalances also make a refusal to make eye contact less reliable as well.

How to make someone drop their guard

When someone likes you, they want to include you in their lives. Listening to what they say often provides deep insight into what controls their lives. People offer up their darkest secrets willingly, believing that I truly understand them.

How you can condition people without their consent/knowledge.

Let's face it; people don't like finding out someone was manipulating them. It violates the idea that we are in control of our lives. But sometimes the truth is hard to take, and we need someone to help us see the way without calling us out on it.

We all manipulate those around us to one degree or another. This can be as simple as breaking a bad habit or establishing new relationship rules with a toxic family member. By steering them in the right direction, we can help them respond to how we prefer.

NLP doesn't brainwash someone (that's covered elsewhere) or cause them to do something out of character. But it does reveal the strings that control each of us. What you do with those strings once you have them is up to you.

Listen and Watch

This is the most time-consuming step, as it is the basis of building the structure for the more intimate relationship you'll build later. Body language is essential to NLP practices. Not only is it vital to the beginning, but, knowing how to read body language comes into play throughout the NLP process and any other psychological process. Luckily, the longer you build a relationship with someone, the easier it will be to know they tell, as they are developed from habit. Some people may be guarded around you, which will appear as tense or straight shoulders and back, not holding your gaze, or even fidgeting. This is a sign you aren't building a vital rapport. Before moving any further, this person needs to feel relaxed and warm around you. Watch for an open face, a relaxed smile, and some easy-going interaction such as light laughter. Stay away from heavy topics until this person is comfortable with you.

Building rapport with others

Every day we use our communications to try and influence others. Unfortunately, most of us are rarely successful because we don't know what we are doing – we don't understand the psychology of other people. We don't know how to get into another person's subconscious mind.

One important aspect of getting on well with others is the building of rapport. First, let's consider what rapport is. Rapport is simple, it is the magic that happens when two people are getting along really well and communicating on the same level. When you have a rapport with another person you are each understanding the other, you are listening better, and you are accomplishing something.

You do not have to think the same way as another person or agree with everything they say to have rapport. You simply have to be communicating similarly. One way that people show rapport is when they mirror each other, that is to say, they have similar body language. People who have a good rapport use a similar body language including posture and eye contact. Imagine in your head that you are talking and laughing with a friend. Likely, you are both standing with your feet a comfortable width apart, your arms moving animatedly as you speak, you are both smiling, and your eyes make frequent contact.

Chapter 2: How To Use Neuro-Linguistic Programming (Nlp)

The most fundamental, basic principle of NLP is positive language. No, I'm not suggesting that by keeping a stiff upper lip, that you might be able to ignore all of your problems—rather, this approach is based in science. You see, the brain is incapable of processing negative language. This means that if you were to tell your communicative partner, "Please do not touch me," what their subconscious mind would be hearing is: "Please do touch me."

According to NLP, your subconscious mind regulates everything from digestion to breathing. This suggests that you are able to communicate with your own subconscious using this technique, as well. The idea is that if you were to repeat, "Do not get well," to yourself as a mantra, your subconscious would only hear, "Do get well," and would respond to this. Of course, negative language is best used in this way on others, and not yourself, because it's entirely possible to just repeat positive mantras to yourself. Many people are unaware of the fact that the subconscious mind is incapable of hearing negative speech (such as 'no' or 'can't'), which makes it even easier to covertly implant ideas into your their subconscious minds without them even being aware that you are the one willing them to act in a certain way.

The only time during which you have to be cognizant of your own internal dialogue when considering the effect of negative language on the subconscious mind is when your self-talk begins using negatives without your awareness. For example, if you accidentally think, "I hope I don't get nervous during this interview," your subconscious mind will hear, "I hope I do get nervous during this interview." For this reason, it is incredibly important to be mindful of the tone of your own internal dialogue, and phrase thoughts positively like, "I hope I am calm during the interview," to bypass negative speech's impact on your brain.

The second most fundamental tenement of using NLP is targeted talk. NLP theorizes that all people communicate in one of three ways: auditory, visual, or kinesthetic. Furthermore, NLP demands of its user to be aware of these communicative styles, and to try to pinpoint which best suits their communicative partner. When your words fit your unique communicative style, it is much easier to deliver new ideas into someone's mind.

The best way to find out someone's communicative style is through listening to them speak. Someone whose style can be described as auditory might use phrases such as: "That sounds great," or "I hear you're busy working on a project." Those who are more prone to kinesthetic communication might say something like: "This homework is hard," or "I feel like you are not listening to me," or even, "I'm going through a rough time." Those who are visual communicators, on the other hand, use phrases like: "I see you went to the shops again this morning," or "Look on the bright side."

Once you determine the style which best fits your communicative partner, you can start using this to your advantage. Visual people are more likely to be complacent if you communicate with them using gestures and smiles. Another great suggestion is to employ vivid, descriptive language to visually express any physical places or things. It is a good idea to do this if you would like to draw your communicative partner in and keep them focused on you.

Auditory people listen to a speaker's tone and intonation. It is thus very important to control the pitch and sound of your voice, using inflections and variances in both to keep your communicative partner engaged.

Kinesthetic learners are 'feelers' and not 'thinkers.' If you can tap into this by using emotive language, instead of just delivering the facts, you're far more likely to be successful in your communications with them. Furthermore, telling them, "I have a gut feeling about this," might make them more prone to believing you, as this is the level that they operate on.

Of course, learning what your communicative partner's communicative style is can take some time, as you would essentially need to build a rapport with them first. Luckily, there is a way to bypass this which is nearly as effective as observing someone's patterns of speech. The trick is to watch their eyes.

Kinesthetic thinkers tend to look down while they are communicating, whilst auditory thinkers look down and visual thinkers look laterally left or right. Watching someone's eye movements might reveal an incredible amount about how they choose to communicate, and how best to communicate with them.

The next NLP technique, which is easy to use and very effective, is known as mirroring. The mirroring technique is based on the idea that we are more prone to trusting people who share similarities with us, such as mannerisms and speech patterns. This means that through careful observation, one might be able to imbibe a few of another person's characteristics. This will eventually help them trust you and share similar perspectives.

The trick with mirroring is to not make it too obvious. If you simply copy your communicative partner's behavior, they'll soon become suspicious and wonder what you are up to. The best way to covertly mirror someone is by matching their speech patterns. If someone is very prone to using slang in their speech, it might be a good idea, for example, to throw some slang words into your own communications with them.

Speech isn't the only thing that can be mirrored, though. Gestures are a good place to start. For example, if your communicative partner is sitting with their legs crossed, you may want to do the same. Here, too, you will need to employ a measure of stealth and not mimic every gesture they make.

Disassociation is another NLP technique that is often used by practitioners. Disassociation cannot usually be used on a communicative partner; instead, its purpose is to help the user overcome negative emotions. These are the steps to follow to employ disassociation:

Identify how you are feeling. Are you feeling sad? Angry? Frustrated? Perhaps scared?

Once you have identified the feeling that you are experiencing, imagine yourself floating out of your body, exiting from the top of your head. Imagine yourself looking down at your body, and seeing its surroundings and how it is reacting to the negative emotion that you wish to eliminate.

Finally, imagine the feeling within yourself changing. Perhaps you feel your chest tightening from nervousness—now imagine feeling that knot in your chest slowly unravel and become loose and comfortable.

Anchoring is the next technique, and this one can be used on communicative partners. Anchoring originated from Ivan Pavlov's theory of classical conditioning. Pavlov conducted an experiment in which he would ring a bell whenever his dogs were eating. After a period of time, Pavlov was able to get the dogs to salivate just by ringing the bell, even when there was no food present. Anchoring works in much the same way.

When using anchoring on a communicative partner, start off by conditioning them with a certain gesture or phrase. Whenever they're experiencing the emotion you would like to elicit in the future, employ this gesture or phrase to connect these two experiences in your communicative partner's mind. If you have been successful in creating an 'anchor,' you should be able to elicit this emotion within your communicative partner simply by using the phrase or gesture in front of them, without any outside stimuli or manipulation.

Another very useful technique is called the "concealed commands" method. A concealed command is a manner of phrasing a question in such a way that your communicative partner does not realize that you are directing him or her toward a set outcome. An example of a concealed command is, "Which movie would you like to watch?" instead of asking, "Would you like to watch a movie?"

The "if you want" technique is somewhat similar to the "concealed commands" method in that they both rely heavily on word play. The purpose of the "if you want" technique is to get your communicative partner to do something which you do not want to do. An example of this is asking your communicative partner, "I can pay the bill if you want"—your communicative partner will feel that since you've offered to pay the bill, etiquette demands they now make the same offer. Which, of course, you will accept. In this way, you're actually shifting the responsibility for the problem onto your communicative partner and away from yourself.

However, word play in NLP doesn't just end and begin with concealed commands and the "if you want" technique. NLP also emphasizes the importance of the word 'but.' 'But' is a special word, because the human mind generally only hears and focuses on the part of the sentence after the 'but.' For example, if I said, "Susan is a pretty girl but she has horrible teeth," all that my communicative partner would hear is that Susan has horrible teeth. If I reworded the question as, "Susan has horrible teeth but she is a pretty girl," all that my communicative partner's mind would absorb is that Susan is a pretty girl.

The opposite is true for the word 'and.' The human mind only hears whatever part of the sentence came before 'and.' This means that if I were to say, "We are going swimming and then we will have lunch," the only thing our mind would focus on is that we are going swimming. However, if I rephrased the sentence to say, "We are going to have lunch, and before that we will go swimming," all the mind would hear is that we are going to have lunch.

Words aren't the only things that hold power in NLP, though. Touch is also important. When you're building a rapport (establishing trust) with a new communicative partner, a few well-placed touches on the upper arm during conversation can lead them into feeling a sense of trust toward you sooner rather than later.

The final NLP technique to be aware of is pacing. Essentially, pacing requires that you give, for example, three definite facts to your communicative partner, followed by the concept which you want your communicative partner to accept as the truth. An example of a pacing script is the following: "Our boss is on leave today (first true fact), and she took the secretaries with her (second true fact). The chief executive officer is here, though (third true fact). Our boss is always on leave (untrue fact)." Because you've prefaced the untrue fact (that your boss is always on leave) by first giving two or three definite facts, your communicative partner is more likely to accept the untrue fact as absolute truth.

Chapter 3: Manipulation

What is manipulation?

People will see the word "manipulation" as a negative or bad image. Whatever method you use to influence someone, you are dealing with him. Every time someone persuades you to do something other than what you want to do, they are really manipulating you.

Manipulation: "Control, Influence, or Manipulation"

Manipulating words have many meanings, some of which can be negative. Being able to handle someone or something is not bad. It can only get worse if you intend to harm or cause trouble. I use word manipulation to do the following:

Control attitudes, beliefs, and behaviors through the self-prescription and self-hypnosis processes Thoughts can affect someone's thoughts and activities. Involved can be moved to an advantageous position for the parties, but this is accepted on both sides. The idea of influencing someone with your own sense of power is as old as civilization. Without going into the full story of hypnosis, trance induction, energy manipulation (available on the internet), I try to give you a good picture An easy-to-understand explanation of what hypnosis and trance are and how to take advantage of them.

1. Artificially induced states of consciousness are characterized by increased direction suggestions and increased acceptance.

The effects of stimulation and hypnosis are like learning a new language

When you begin to apply and apply the principles of this book, you will need to enter a "time of flight." This means that you need to register for a special purpose to achieve the desired results of the training.

There are many ways you can learn to construct languages and sentences that actually transcend your current language. To understand the meaning of the idea taught, you need to stretch.

Psychological examination: Must look like an actor

When actors appear in front of the stage or camera, do they create lines or use scripts?

Each actor uses a script to learn his line. The same is true when you start learning how to influence or enforce taxes. You need to practice the line (time of flight) many times to get the methods and concepts in your head.

You have to do the same because the actor embraces the person for the role he plays. You need to get out of the current comfort zone, out of the box, and start walking.

To restrain someone is simply or unreasonably restrictive or affecting. Like us or not, we all manipulate people and situations to achieve the desired outcome.

It sounds dark but excites my naughty childhood story. When I didn't want to go to school as a kid, I got sick. First of all, my parents kept typing me up whenever this happened. After two hasty trips to the clinic, my mother doubted my sports symptoms. The next few times, they did not take me to the clinic, but they allowed me to stay at home. During an episode of my stomach, a friend of mine excitedly told me that a local actor was attending school. I ran to my mom and asked her to take her to school, but forgot that "stomach pain is unbearable." My mother told me she didn't take any chances, and I was there. There were no demands or excuses that could change his mind after admitting that she acted like a stomach ache. When I came to school the next day, my friend showed me all the wonderful things the actor had brought and could envy. Suffice it to say that you never found a cure for leaving school.

This story is just one of many stories of what we do to deal with the situation. I still know many adults who pretend to be cold and retire from work. Isn't that bad? Sometimes we work to make useful choices for us. Your friend will provide you with the best sneakers and monthly plan at the local gym. You know you need to strengthen your fitness department. Have you ever had lunch with a friend to reach the expected date and sudden emergencies (for your friends, of course)? I was there. One of the ways we can get out of this unpleasant situation is when we feel threatened

Power is not an option, and it is a function.

In other words, functional art is part of our nature. But when it comes to psychological manipulation, things get dark. In this situation, a person's behavior or thinking is affected by the use of covert tactics that are aggressive, misleading, or both. In this context, the handled person cannot accept or reject the handler's will. They are simply implemented.

The handler has a reason to execute. Sometimes, as simple as a fictional soldier making financial profits disappointed all of my neighbors' savings in life. At work, these people are determined to promote their agenda, even if that means wiping some heads off each other. The principle is very simple. If you want to, you have to achieve it. In a relationship, this is usually performance control. The need to take responsibility promotes everything they do, and sometimes they can make great efforts to achieve it. Some people want to manipulate people for entertainment purposes. You get bored and manipulate time with the surgical game. It's gross and evil, but that's their way of thinking.

One of the most common manipulator's tricks is lies. Master manipulators can cheat well. They are good at bringing out great stories without affecting the truth. Or they move and lie by letting go. Some people can lie so well that they only notice the lie when it's too late. Another tactic used by manipulators is to cause guilt and shame. If you encounter a mistake, you immediately contest it and then immediately turn the tables so that you are fed up with doubting it. Nor do they trust that the victims will strengthen their hold and make them abusers. This type of manipulation technique is found in domestic cases where the perpetrator states that the victim's character, language, or act originally triggered his or her actions.

Other advanced techniques used for manipulation include using avoidable uncertain answers to questions. Optimize the captured actions and turn reality to fit the story. Some manipulators use sex and seduction to achieve the worst of their intentions. If their hands get caught in the proverbial "cookie jar," anger and guilt are used to quickly manipulate the situation. However, handlers are not always random when choosing prey.

Victims have certain characteristics that attract them, and some victims are more likely to commit crimes. It is easier to control the individual who is ready for poor self-esteem and happiness than certain social types. However, some have properties similar to the latter. For such individuals, the manipulators will analyze their personality before using it against their weaknesses and weaknesses. Impressive individuals can be fooled by their appearance. Those who are brave enough to make compelling decisions are more likely to be manipulated to make quick decisions that have lasting consequences. Greed and materialists are more likely to be fooled.

1. They make you guilty for everything.

Surgery always starts with guilt. If they can convince you of guilt about your actions (even if you have not made a mistake), they know that you will be more satisfied with what they say. "Of course, dinner was just right. It wasn't what I expected. Instead, I would have done something different. But I think it's important as long as you're happy."

Do you see what they did there? How did they make it to you? On the surface, they look like loving partners, but spoilers notice: guilt is not loved.

The manipulator makes you believe that you are doing the wonderful job of "I love you" and is ready to put aside what you want to feel. "How much you love it." It is a sick mind game.

2. They are worried about you.

Handlers often annoy the user to control what to do. "I've been cheered on before, so I don't want to have friends of the opposite sex (or same-sex, sexual orientation). You see?" Yes, of course, you can understand it (and you should know their fear), but their struggle shouldn't define the function of your relationship.

"Sorry, I acted this way, but I'm very afraid that you will leave me!" This is an excuse that handlers often use when they point out errors in the action. The real purpose of this reason is to distract your worries and absorb them for you.

See Tango Relationship Advice

There is a fine line between looking at their emotions and manipulating what you want them to feel. Considerations for dealing with guilt are made.

3. They make you doubt yourself.

Would you like to know why it is so easy to use? Because they brainwashed you too much, you no longer believe in yourself. Yes, handlers take your fears and use them against you. They always indicate that you are "doing it wrong" and how they could be better. They point out your weaknesses and show that with their help, you can always improve. I think they're starting to take their best interests into account, but they're not.

You have the best interests in mind. To keep their desires and needs at the forefront of your relationship, slow down your thinking until you turn to him for all the instructions. Once this happens, the manipulator can do whatever you want.

4. They make you responsible for their emotions.

Manipulators are contradictory, so it takes some time before you feel like you can't think of yourself, but you turn around and take responsibility for all your emotions. If they were sad, you would probably have made them feel that way. If you are angry, do something wrong and check it yourself.

You expect yourself to be responsible for how you feel if you believe that you cannot fully control your own life, no matter how far away you are.

5. Make them believe that you want them.

We all initiate relationships with requirements and breaches of contract. It is natural to mix two endangered lives what is normal: when you have to put aside what you need and what you need to be happy with your partner. If you feel that your partner's needs are being met more often than you, you may be married to a manipulator.

Do they achieve what they want out of guilt, or do they blame you for how you feel? Did you leave because you wanted something else? If you answer "yes" to these questions, you can reassess the relationship.

Chapter 4: The Dark Triad

Remorse, Regret, and Sorry are three words essential to adaptive living. These three words when practiced boost the probability of all social interactions achieving success. Ignorance and/or refusal of the mental triad cause criminal and/or deviant habits with victimization as the modus operandi. Two diminutive words, "I'm Sorry", is just one of the most effective and intricate phrases uttered in communication.

Since the start of civilization, this phrase has become part of all societal and cultural exchanges communicated through various languages. "I'm Sorry" will always be essential to social relationships. The premise of this expression concretely highlights how all people are fallible beings. Actions and/or words can anger briefly or inflict a long-lasting psychological scar void of healing. Understanding the meaning and origins of "I'm Sorry" will assist the reader in understanding this effective phrase.

The actual term, Sorry, goes back to ancient times and theorized to stem from the West Germanic term, Sairig, a derivative of Sairaz, with the English source representing Sore. The original definition meant both physical and mental pain. Over hundreds of years, the word developed into an expression of remorse now used as what we say..., Sorry. Regardless of the resemblance, the word Sorry has no etymological connection with the term, Sorrow. This word also goes back to ancient Germanic language indicating "care."

The term, Sorry, is an adjective with a wide range of meanings defining different interactions uttered in social relationships. From a reductionist viewpoint, and adding the identifier, I'm, makes the expression a type of apology and expression of regret.

The meaning of apology is an expression of remorse for causing another person trouble or real pain. The definition of remorse means to feel remorse or contrite about one's actions. Regret and remorse are two feelings people, in general, have a really difficult time experiencing and admitting.

Regret is another crucial term to succinctly comprehend the phrase, "I'm Sorry." Without the experience of remorse, it is unrealistic to truly communicate remorse for ones misdeed(s). Remorse is defined as a sense of deep remorse and regret for causing a person harm. Depending on the damage committed, the seriousness of regret can range from subtle to extreme. The societal purpose of remorse is to educate people on habits that are not acceptable in social interactions.

Without the experience of regret, people can't learn to change their actions leading to a more favorable lifestyle. Since the beginning of recorded history, society has written poetry, music, tunes, and different other forms of communication in an attempt to specify and reveal the experience of regret. Without remorse for wrongdoings, civilization could not exist and isolation would be crucial to human existence.

Human beings are social beings making it through and growing within a group dynamic. As part of the evolutionary structure, remorse and communication of remorse are both urged and necessary for the survival of all people, the humankind.

Given the vital purpose of remorse and regret to mankind, the term, "I'm Sorry", is often confused by suspicions of sincerity. An individual's character and integrity is a barometer of genuineness and the effect of communicating regret is directly linked to the person's intent. If integrity is deemed suspect, then attempts to ask forgiveness can easily be interpreted as misguided devoid of sincerity.

Character and integrity associated to being genuinely sorry is connected to past, present, and future actions following their misbehaviour(s). Some are unforgivable while most are accepted provided particular actions are exhibited after her/his misdeed(s). The end item of actions following a misdeed is freshly learned habits reducing the potential for repetition of the specific misbehaviours.

An analogy to show human fallibility not addressed, changed, or redirected would be the person who struggles with alcohol addiction. Although the alcoholic is secretly aware his or her drinking triggers real pain and anguish to others, he or she continues to drink using a variety of defense mechanisms like denial, displacement, and reduction. Engaged in the progressive demise of her or his character, integrity, and trust by others, the alcoholic may go years right before experiencing remorse and avoiding future alcohol consumption. The procedure of recognition, remorse, regret, recovery, and rehabilitation shows the course all people should experience in the process of positive human adaptation.

Without remorse or regret for actions considered hurtful by others, the likelihood of positive change is tiny. Given the depths of the human mind, there are generous defense mechanisms ready to protect someone from feeling remorse for their actions. The capability to say, "I'm Sorry", and mean it requires an internal reservoir called conscience. Conscience is specified as a moral sense of right and very wrong. This psychological construct affects an individual's behavior and motivates the functioning behavior.

Awareness, thinking, awareness, and self-awareness are all pertinent aspects of the conscience. This construct is a lot like a glass of water ranging from empty to full. Most people's reservoir of conscience varieties from 1/2 to 3/4 filled. As pointed out above, a part of the human condition is fallibility and predisposition to engage in nonfunctional conduct(s). The less conscience an individual has, the more apt he or she is at a threat for victimizing others. The severest result of lacking a vessel of conscience would be the criminal, deviant, or sociopathic mind.

The expression, "I'm Sorry", is just one of the most important phrases associated with the human experience. From the start of time and advertisement infinitum afterwards, the procedure of recognition, regret, remorse, and rehab will always be a barometer for human adaptability. Laws, religions, viewpoints, and familial guidelines for raising children are all tailored to manage and lower human suffering.

The objective is quite easy and easy to practice using 5 steps.

1. Expect others to become offended given the variability of perceptions filtering all human interactions.

2. Whether innocent or guilty causing others harm, initiate an apology followed by empathy for their experience.

3. Explain in words a plan for not upsetting in the future.

4. Introspect on and start a paradigm shift decreasing the potential for future angering action(s).

5. Never forget, always forgive, and foster mutual respect.

Chapter 5: What Is Neuro-Linguistics?

Neurolinguistics is the investigation of the neural components in the human mind that control the cognizance, creation, and obtaining of language. As an interdisciplinary field, neurolinguistics draws techniques and speculations from fields, for example, neuroscience, semantics, subjective science, correspondence issue and neuropsychology. Analysts are attracted to the field from an assortment of foundations, bringing along an assortment of trial procedures just as broadly fluctuating hypothetical points of view. Much work in neurolinguistics is educated by models in psycholinguistics and hypothetical phonetics, and is centered around exploring how the mind can execute the procedures that hypothetical and psycholinguistics propose are essential in creating and understanding language. Neurolinguists study the physiological components by which the cerebrum forms data identified with language, and assess phonetic and psycholinguistic hypotheses, utilizing aphasiology, mind imaging, electrophysiology, and PC demonstrating.

Neurolinguistics is generally established in the improvement in the nineteenth century of aphasiology, the investigation of phonetic shortfalls (aphasias) happening as the consequence of mind harm. Aphasiology endeavors to connect structure to work by dissecting the impact of mind wounds on language preparing. One of the principal individuals to draw an association between a specific mind territory and language preparing was Paul Broca, a French specialist who directed post-mortem examinations on various people who had talking lacks, and found that a large portion of them had cerebrum harm (or sores) on the left frontal projection, in a zone currently known as Broca's zone. Phrenologists had made the case in the mid nineteenth century that diverse mind areas did various capacities and that language was for the most part constrained by the frontal districts of the cerebrum, yet Broca's examination was perhaps the first to offer exact proof for such a relationship, and has been portrayed as "age making" and "vital" to the fields of neurolinguistics and intellectual science. Afterward, Carl Wernicke, after whom Wernicke's region is named, suggested that various territories of the cerebrum were specific for various phonetic errands, with Broca's region dealing with the engine creation of discourse, and Wernicke's territory taking care of sound-related discourse perception. The field of aphasiology and the possibility that language can be contemplated through looking at physical qualities of the cerebrum. Early work in aphasiology likewise profited by the mid twentieth-century work of Korbinian Brodmann, who "mapped" the outside of the mind, splitting it into numbered territories dependent on every region's cytoarchitecture (cell structure) and capacity; these zones, known as Brodmann regions, are still broadly utilized in neuroscience today.

The begetting of the expression "neurolinguistics" is ascribed to Edith Crowell Trager, Henri Hecaen and Alexandr Luria, in the late 1940s and 1950s; Luria's book "Issues in Neurolinguistics" is likely the primary book with Neurolinguistics in the title. Harry Whitaker promoted neurolinguistics in the United States during the 1970s, establishing the diary "Cerebrum and Language" in 1974.

Despite the fact that aphasiology is the verifiable center of neurolinguistics, as of late the field has widened impressively, thanks to a limited extent to the development of new mind imaging advancements, (for example, PET and fMRI) and time-touchy electrophysiological strategies (EEG and MEG), which can feature examples of cerebrum enactment as individuals take part in different language assignments; electrophysiological systems, specifically, rose as a feasible strategy for the investigation of language in 1980 with the disclosure of the N400, a cerebrum reaction demonstrated to be delicate to semantic issues in language cognizance. The N400 was the main language-applicable occasion related potential to be recognized, and since its revelation EEG and MEG have gotten progressively broadly utilized for directing language inquire about.

Communication with different fields

Neurolinguistics is firmly identified with the field of psycholinguistics, which looks to explain the intellectual systems of language by utilizing the customary strategies of exploratory brain science; today, psycholinguistic and neurolinguistic hypotheses frequently advise each other, and there is a lot of cooperation between the two fields.

Much work in neurolinguistics includes testing and assessing speculations set forth by psycholinguists and hypothetical language specialists. As a rule, hypothetical etymologists propose models to clarify the structure of language and how language data is sorted out, psycholinguists propose models and calculations to clarify how language data is handled in the brain, and neurolinguists break down mind movement to surmise how organic structures (populaces and systems of neurons) complete those psycholinguistic preparing calculations. For instance, tests in sentence preparing have utilized the ELAN, N400, and P600 mind reactions to analyze how physiological cerebrum reactions mirror the various expectations of sentence handling models set forth by psycholinguists, "sequential" model, and Theo Vosse and Gerard Kempen's "unification model". Neurolinguists can likewise make new expectations about the structure and association of language dependent on bits of knowledge about the physiology of the cerebrum, by "summing up from the information on neurological structures to language structure". Neurolinguistics inquire about is done in all the significant territories of semantics; the fundamental etymological subfields, and how neurolinguistics tends to them, are given in the table underneath.

The Interdisciplinary Nature of Neurolinguistics

Which controls must be considered in neurolinguistics? Mind and Language expresses that its interdisciplinary center incorporates the fields of etymology, neuroanatomy, nervous system science, neurophysiology, theory, brain research, psychiatry, discourse pathology, and software engineering. These controls might be the ones generally associated with neurolinguistics however a few different orders are likewise profoundly significant, having added to speculations, strategies, and discoveries in neurolinguistics. They incorporate neurobiology, humanities, science, psychological science, and computerized reasoning. In this way, the humanities, and medicinal, common, and sociologies, just as innovation are altogether spoken to.

Co-advancement of Language and the Brain

It is uncontroversial, in logical circles in any event, that the human mind has experienced exceptionally quick development in late advancement. The cerebrum has multiplied in size in under one million years. The reason for this 'runaway' development (Wills, 1993) involves guess and interminable discussion. A solid case can be made that the extension of the cerebrum was an outcome of the improvement of communicated in language and the endurance advantage that having a language presents. The territories of the mind that experienced most prominent improvement have all the earmarks of being explicitly connected with language: the frontal flaps and the intersection of the parietal, occipital and worldly projections.

Neurolinguistics and Research in Speech Production

The idea of neurolinguistic programs has pulled in a lot of research as of late, particularly in connection to discourse creation. It is apparent, for instance, that the cerebrum doesn't give engine directions each portion in turn. . . . At the point when we consider the entire scope of variables that influence the planning of discourse occasions, (for example, breathing rate, the development and coordination of the articulators, the beginning of vocal-crease vibration, the area of stress, and the position and span of stops), it is apparent that a profoundly refined control framework must be utilized, generally discourse would decline into an inconsistent, disordered arrangement of commotions. It is currently perceived that numerous zones of the cerebrum are included: specifically, the cerebellum and thalamus are known to help the cortex in practicing this control. In any case, it isn't yet conceivable to build a definite model of neurolinguistic activity that considers all discourse generation factors.

Envision how enormous your cerebrum is and its numerous experiences with various musings daily. You cerebrum is choose a breakdown regardless of whether you don't care for it when it has arrived at its farthest point. Regardless of whether confirmations or reactions are being stated, our minds hold it. The main contrast is reactions will in general last more and infuriates our regard. It seriously influences our presentation in our every day lives and thus, we fall flat. Every single one of us experience adrenaline surge when you like something and that adrenaline censuring when somebody said you are bad enough. Some endeavor to be better yet a few tumbles down together with their aspiration. Word is an incredible asset that we can utilize either to elevate or crash our own and another person's soul. In the event that yours has been smashed down, this is the ideal opportunity to recapture it. Regarding Neurolinguistic, the main utilization of language is to imbue constructive contemplations into an individual's brain.

Neurolinguistic means to change the plan of an individual's conduct. It could assist an individual with making out of his/her potential and show to the world that he/she can take on anything. Essentially, the extent of the program is to ponder the individual's conduct and reinvent it through reaching the mind. This sort of approach is once in a while called as the "study of greatness" due to suitable treatment for primary issues, for example, fears, issue and the preferences. These issues hinder the development of an individual as it were that they are reluctant to go past their usual range of familiarity. By investigating, you can find yourself and your restrictions that is the reason you truly need to peel off that area of you that is terrified.

On and when you consider looking at Neurolinguistic, it will open you up in the realm of Amazement. It is unquestionably the harmony that you are wanting for. Envision. No fears or disarranges so implies opportunity. Opportunity to dream, find and accomplish. Your assurance emerges in light of the fact that your certainty is helped. You can become whoever you need to be and get anything you desire to have. In that sense, you can call it flawless life.

Try not to block yourself. Be bold and play. Since just you have control of what you can turn into.

In the event that you need to enable your brain, to liberate it based on what is confining it inside. Since it is such a great amount of better to live outside you safe place. There are things yet to find, love yet to give and individuals yet to meet. On and when you are apprehensive, that is ordinary yet search out for ways that can give you a chance to live better, since you merit it. We all merit it. On and when you believe that past is frustrating you, desert it since future is a lot of significant than the past. It is something that is intended for us to design, decide and accomplish. So put out your peddle and sketch your future above all, you have to liberate yourself based on what is keeping you down.

Neurolinguistics, the investigation of the neurological systems basic the capacity and handling of language. In spite of the fact that it has been decently agreeably discovered that the language focus is in the left side of the equator of the mind in right-gave individuals, debate remains concerning whether singular parts of language are corresponded with various specific regions of the cerebrum. One sort of research carried on in this field is the investigation of aphasia, a state of the cerebrum where language capacity is disabled or devastated. Brief aphasia has been incited by electrically animating the cortex of cognizant patients so as to decide the area of the different elements of language. Albeit exceptionally broad focuses of language have been proposed, it appears that there are no profoundly specific focuses. A few cases have been accounted for of patients who, in the wake of having their left side of the equator of the mind expelled, adjusted in the correct half of the globe the language work that the left side of the equator had. When all is said in done, nonetheless, however progress is being made in this field, next to no is known for sure about the neurological parts of language.

Chapter 6: Understanding Psychopaths

Psychopaths have three parts of the dark triad, they are easily at the top of the list for whom to look out for, especially if you yourself are not one. However, the first interesting thing to note is that while all psychopaths are narcissistic, narcissists are not necessarily going to be psychopathic. Knowing this may be one of the weaknesses that may allow you to spot a psychopath if you find yourself crossing paths with one.

Psychopathy is identified as Antisocial Personality Disorder (APD). It has a lot of characteristics that, similar to narcissism, tend to be misconstrued by the public. This is often due to ignorance or misinformation, like that of the psychotic serial killer one sees in Hollywood movies. While this image isn't entirely untrue, largely due to the fact that these people are the most likely within the dark triad to become abusers and serial killers, many psychopaths are actually very good at blending into society. In fact, psychopaths are often well educated and intelligent.

Regardless of how well they blend into society, there is a way to help unearth the truth about them. Firstly, they will often have the same grandiose sense of self mixed in with compulsive lying and highly manipulative behavior that shows no regard for morality or the wellbeing of others. For one thing, research shows that they tend to be born the way they are. This means that your average psychopath educated or not, will probably show a history of bad behavior from an early age. They may even have a criminal record.

Examples of psychopaths from the history

Brain scans carried out on psychopaths show that the parts of the brain that are activated when most people feel stress, guilt, or empathy remain inactive when they are given stimuli that are meant to trigger these kinds of feelings(MedCircle, 2018). Their very autonomic system (which is largely responsible for reflective responses like the fight or flight and the immune system etc.) are wired differently from most peoples. Depending on the kind of psychopath, you will find that they often excel and be found in higher concentrations in occupations such as lawyers, stockbrokers, assassins, salespeople, surgeons and (quite surprisingly) chefs.

What how do they operate?

High functioning- while people think that the term psychopathy is monolithic, it actually has two subcategories that are important to understand if one is to know what to look out for. The first of these being the high functioning psychopath.

These people are just more controlled and calculating. They are far less likely to become serial killers and rather channel that energy into something else, like their careers. In fact, these kinds of psychopaths are far more likely to be seen occupying high power jobs like CEOs of companies.

Don't think this makes them anything like the rest of society. These people are still vicious predators who will eliminate anyone in their way with a ruthlessness most people are not capable of. They aren't afraid to go as far as commit murder or ruin a business at the cost of countless people losing their livelihoods. They are incapable of remorse or shame and will not lose any sleep over their actions.

Low functioning- these are more the types we see in the slasher movies in theatres. The low functioning psychopath usually has a much more difficult time managing their instincts and emotions, so they are far more likely to become serial killers. However, they just don't operate the way most people would imagine.

They are more likely to draw their victims in with charm, or glibness. This is when they prepare to ruin their target's life. They are still calculating, but don't have the ability to redirect those instincts the way their high functioning counterparts do.

They still tend to be very good at concealing their true selves under a veil of normalcy. They are great liars, so leading a double life is not difficult for them. They are typically also well educated, so hiding their actions is no great feat since psychopaths generally seem to be intelligent people. So don't count on them giving themselves away so easily.

What can we learn from them?

Now as dangerous as the psychopath might be, regardless of their specific brand of crazy, they are not to be ignored. They have a lot to teach, especially for those who are looking for upward mobility in life. These skilled predators among us are good to study for multiple reasons, the most obvious one probably being one's own safety.

While they only make up about 1% of any given population, you will find that it still makes a lot of people when you consider how many people there are on planet earth. This means that there is a very good chance that everyone will meet at least one psychopath in their life. So it probably for the best that you knows how to identify them and act accordingly for your own best interest and for that of those close to you.

One of the best things we can learn from psychopaths is their ability to detach their emotions from any action. While this cannot be mastered to the same degree by most people, it can be adopted to a certain extent. Finding detachment from the things and people around us can be a great end in itself. One does not need to become cold to everything and everyone they know and love. It is good enough that one simply learn to embrace solitude so that they can focus more on their own self-interest.

Psychopaths are not easily affected by stress. This gives them the ability to calmly assess any given situation and act accordingly. What's more, they are not as likely to suffer from paralysis by analysis. Their autonomic systems are a big part of the reason they are so unmoved by taking risks.

Chapter 7: Safeguarding Yourself From Dark Psychologists

Being aware of the ways that people may manipulate you is only one way to safeguard yourself from dark psychologists. There are also techniques that you can use to make yourself less vulnerable. By using the strategies in this chapter, dark psychologists will be less likely to prey on you. They may notice that you are aware of their tactics and realize that you are not worth their time, as you will not be as susceptible to their efforts as someone else.

Protecting Yourself from Manipulators

Even when you learn to identify people practicing dark psychology, some may be sneaky enough to slip under your radar. By using the techniques in this section, you can guard yourself even when you have not yet identified someone as a dark psychologist.

#1: Know When You Are Most Vulnerable

Dark psychologists pride themselves in knowing the perfect moment to strike. They may wait until you are tired at the end of a long day before asking you for something, knowing that if they ramble on enough, you will cave just for some peace. They may also target you when you are busy or stressed since you will have other things on your mind and be less likely to notice their techniques. Even though it is easy to let your guard down when you already have so much on your plate, these are the times when you need to safeguard yourself the most. Be wary of people in your life who always try to ask questions at the worst times—they may be trying to catch you with your guard down.

#2: Move Your Eyes Randomly

Dark psychologists often seem like they are watching you intensely. Even though this might come off as showing interest, it is much more likely that they are paying close attention to your eye movements. People who have studied neuro-linguistic programming may be familiar with the way the eyes naturally move when you are accessing information in your brain. By paying attention to the movements, someone could learn how you access certain information and use it to manipulate you at a later time. To prevent this, make it a habit of moving your eyes randomly as you talk. Let them dart up, down, and to the sides. You should do this in a natural way, but the random pattern stops the other person from gaining insight about your thought processes.

#3: Pay Attention to Body Language

A common strategy used by salespeople and those who want to influence is to mimic someone else's body language. Usually, they wait 2-3 seconds before copying each of your movements in a subtle way. When this mimicry goes unnoticed, it leads the person being mimicked to think highly of the person, because they believe they are more alike. This is successful because it slips past the consciousness and sinks into the subconscious mind. Move your hand a certain way when you are talking to someone and then watch. If they mimic you, wait a few moments before doing something else. If they mimic you again, call them out. Watch them become flustered as they realize their efforts were in vain.

#4: Notice Language

When someone uses vague language, they are generally trying to slip past the defenses of your mind. By avoiding words that you can disagree with, the vague language can introduce a hypnotic state. Get in the habit of asking for clarity. If a person cannot provide clarity, then you know they were trying to trick you.

Permissive language also poses a problem. They may tell you that you are 'free' to go for a test drive or that you 'can' relax. This is meant as a suggestion, but generally, people follow it. By granting permission, they lead you to that decision while allowing you to believe that you reached the conclusion on your own.

#5: Avoid Physical Contact

Physical contact can be used as an anchor for emotional states. For example, if you are excited or angry about something and someone touches you on the arm, they are anchoring you to that state. You relate that heightened emotional state with the physical touch, so all they have to do if they want you to become excited or angry again is touch you in the same place.

#6: Trust Your Intuition

People have trouble going with their gut feelings, especially if they are commonly criticized for being nervous or anxious about situations. If you are worried that someone is taking advantage of you, trust your gut feeling. People who are practicing neuro-linguistic programming, manipulation, and other dark psychology techniques are subtle, trying to leave little evidence of what they are attempting to do. Don't wait for them to take advantage of you before you distance yourself.

#7: Don't Make Rushed Decisions

Putting pressure on someone is the easiest way to get them to make a rash decision. When you do not have the time to think about something and process it fully, you are more likely to say 'yes.' Instead, make it a habit of waiting 24 hours before making a decision. When a coworker insists that you have to go out and get drinks to celebrate after work, tell them you need a rain check and you will let them know what is going on tomorrow. Wait at least a day before going back to a car lot and deciding if the vehicle you test drove is worth it. When people are trying to benefit themselves, they will rush you to get you to go along with what they want. Don't let them make you feel as if you do not have time to clear your head or do the research.

#8: Observe Them with Others

People who practice dark psychology have more than one side to their personality. While they may be smooth and charming with one person, they may use fear tactics to get their way with another. There is not a specific method—they just use what works best on a per-case basis. Keep in mind that even though someone seems incredibly charismatic when they are around you, it does not always mean this is the reality of their personality. Pay close attention to how they interact with other people when you are not around. Through careful observation, you may find contradicting behaviors in their repertoire that indicate they are using manipulative tactics to get the things they want.

#9: Get Evidence

Manipulators thrive on the fact that you do not have evidence that they said (or did not say) something. When you have to deal with someone at work who tries to twist other people's words or make you look like the bad guy, start discreetly recording conversations. Alternatively, you can write down the things that they say. Recording would provide more evidence if you are trying to have the person reprimanded, especially if they are using threatening or fear tactics to get their way.

Otherwise, writing is just fine. The record is more supposed to be used for your peace of mind, letting you review the details of your conversation even when they deny that they said something. This will help you stop them from justifying poor behavior at a later time.

#10: Catch Them Off Guard

When manipulators are using one of their more negative tactics, return with a positive rebuttal. For example, imagine that two coworkers are giving a presentation as to why they should be promoted to manager. The manipulator approaches the other woman applying for the job and tells her that her dress is unattractive or outdated, in an attempt to shake her confidence. Rather than letting the manipulator win or showing weakness, the woman might respond by saying, "I know. It was my mother's dress though and I always feel super confident when I wear it." As you continue to respond to negative attacks with positivity, it becomes more likely that the dark psychologist will take a hint and leave you alone. You will not be worth their time or energy.

#11: Avoid Emotional Attachment

The reason many people fall into the trap of being in a relationship with a narcissist or psychopath is that they rarely show their true colors at first. They consciously decide to manipulate people, but these are not traits that are shared the first few times you meet someone. This makes it hard to stop emotional attachment, especially if you know someone for a while before you realize that they are manipulating you. If at all possible, however, you should break things off early. Know that manipulators commonly have more than one target. If you break things off before they can really get into your head, they will become distracted with their next target and leave you alone.

#12: Nip Drama in the Bud

Telling someone they are right is easier said than done. When a dark psychologist is trying to get you to see their perspective, however, you may find yourself in an hour-long argument over who is right. They are fueled by the drama and will never concede on their opinion, which makes it a waste of energy to continue trying to persuade them of your point. Instead of acting confrontationally the next time a manipulator approaches you, tell them "You're right." While this is not necessarily the easiest thing for your ego, it does give you the opportunity to walk away. You do not fuel the manipulator's fire, so they may be less likely to target you in the future.

#13: Meditate Daily

Mediation has a number of benefits for the body and mind. However, it is also a useful tool that can help protect you from dark psychologists. When you meditate regularly, you are more in tune with your intuition and your own emotions. This means you may be more likely to follow your gut instinct when it is telling you that something is not right with another person. Additionally, meditating regularly gives you a sense of inner peace. Even if the manipulator is trying to incite chaos around you, you can be confident that your inner peace will help you get through that chaos. As you do not feed their need for drama, you will also find that the manipulator eventually moves on to an easier and more satisfying target.

#14: Get Perspective

There are many people who will insist that change is possible. While this is true, change is something that must be motivated from deep within. People who practice dark psychology intentionally do not have an inner drive to be a better person. Even though some may have experienced a rough childhood or other circumstances that have caused them to be this way, it does not mean that they are willing to change. While you might be able to influence change by being a positive role model and meeting the manipulator's combativeness with kindness, you should not go out of your way to do so. Keep your distance even if they say they are willing to change.

#16: Keep Your Mood Up

Dark psychologists thrive on dragging down the people around them. They nitpick at their flaws and insecurities until they find a way to make them unravel. When you find yourself with a negative feeling you cannot shake, make it a habit to give yourself a positivity boost. Keep a few pieces of your favorite chocolate handy so you can indulge yourself for a much-needed boost. You can also take a few minutes to meditate or speak positively to yourself to boost your mood. If these things do not work, try getting a laugh. Laughing releases endorphins that naturally improve your mood.

#17: Be Aware of Acts of Power

All types of people who practice dark psychology have one thing in common—a need to be in control. They may use different strategies to achieve this control, however, they must develop it if they are to influence the people around them. People who are manipulative often exaggerate their ability to control those around them. In some cases, even though they are exaggerating, they actually believe that they can bend everyone around them to their will. This is when dark psychologists become dangerous, as the belief that they can manipulate anyone may lead them to do things that are unethical or illegal because they believe they are superior and can get away with it. In addition to believing they have power, it is not uncommon for them to act as if they have power. They may become loud or aggressive when not getting their way, believing that acting in this way increases their control. When things do not go as planned, their sense of entitlement pushes them over the top.

Removing Manipulators from Your Life

Aside from being aware of manipulators, what should you do when you encounter one in your life? A big mistake people make is thinking that they can fix a manipulator. Many of the people who practice dark psychology cannot be fixed. Think back to the example of sociopaths and the way that their brain scans compared to those of 'normal' people—they were much less responsive. Additionally, even if manipulators convince you that they want to change, it is unlikely this is not another ploy. They will not change—they will just get more crafty at using strategies to manipulate you. Use these strategies as you work to remove those people whose only focus is themselves from your life:

1. Expect to Be Manipulated and Protect Yourself

Something that you should expect when confronting a dark psychologist is to be manipulated. It is not uncommon for manipulators to threaten to kill themselves or harm themselves in some way once you tell them that you are not interested in a friendship/relationship. Some may even threaten your well-being—this is something that should be taken seriously. Speak to the police and keep yourself safe. Even though most psychopaths and sociopaths are not dangerous, there are enough dangerous people that it is worth taking the extra precaution.

#2: Know When to Keep Your Distance

In some cases, it is best not to bring up a person's manipulative habits. For example, it is likely that someone who is manipulative can charm your boss enough that they are cleared of your suspicions. When you cannot stay away completely, get in the habit of keeping your distance. Try to avoid working with that person when you do not have to. Choose to be friends with different social circles than them when you are at work.

#3: Refuse to Compromise

The art of compromise is a great skill. Unfortunately, when used by a manipulator, it is just another tactic for them to exercise control over you. For example, when you are dating someone and break things off because they are manipulative, they may try to convince you to change. They might ask you to wait a month while they start attending therapy or working on their issues, then beg for you to give them one more chance. This is a way for them to continue keeping you close—do not fall for it. Odds are, they will not attend therapy or try to better themselves during that time anyway.

#4: Don't Feel Guilty

It is easy to feel guilty when someone is feigning pain, especially since you are not a psychopath or sociopath. You should not feel guilty when you break things off with a manipulator. Regardless of how special they make you feel, they will move onto targeting someone else. They often depend on other people to give them the attention they crave. Even when a manipulator threatens to harm themselves, you cannot give in. They want you to feel guilty enough that you let them continue manipulating you. If you are truly concerned, call an ambulance or the police. Once you cut ties, they are no longer your responsibility—no matter how close you thought you were to the person.

#5: Prepare for Personal Attacks

Master manipulators get in your head so they know your weaknesses and insecurities. By knowing the parts of yourself that you struggle with the most, they gain the ability to pick apart your flaws. This is a technique used to decrease your self-confidence. When you try to break things off, do not be surprised when the dark psychologist starts hurling insults and insisting they cannot be replaced. They are trying to unsettle you enough that you give into what they want.

People who use dark psychology are counting on you to let your guard down so they can manipulate your mind. There is no limit to the number of strategies they can and will employ to get the things they want. Keep in mind that being aware of your surroundings and your interactions with people are your best defense against mental manipulation.

Chapter 8: Manipulation

Where It Comes From, How It's Used, and How to Avoid It

Manipulation. It's a word we hear all the time, usually in regard to personal relationships.

"He was really manipulative."

"I'm so glad I got out of that manipulative relationship."

But what does it mean? Where are the origins of manipulation in human nature? Why and how do we use it? How can we recognize and avoid when it's being used against us?

It's Psychological

When we talk about manipulation in this context, what we are really talking about is psychological manipulation. This type of manipulation is defined as having a social or psychological influence over another person or group. Social influence in and of itself is not necessarily harmful or fall under the category of dark psychology. Psychological manipulation seeks to change the perceptions or behaviors of its subject, to fulfill the desires of the manipulator.

Manipulation can also be a two-way street between the manipulator and the manipulated. People who are vulnerable to being manipulated also validate the manipulator's actions, which cycles back into a greater desire to feel that power over the manipulated.

Using Manipulation

Two basic theories have been popularized about the use of manipulation and the character of the people who use it. The first theory was developed by forensic psychologist George K. Simon. Simon believes that true manipulation is achieved through the use of covert aggressiveness. His theory holds that there are three things a manipulator must know in order to be successful:

1- How to conceal their true intentions;

2- How to determine their subject's weaknesses and vulnerabilities; and

3- How to brush aside any feelings of guilt or remorse at their actions.

According to Dr. Simon, manipulators use a large number of techniques to undermine their subjects, many of which we'll cover in-depth later in this book. Simon's list of manipulative tactics includes, but is not exclusive to:

Lies and lies of omission (deception), rationalization and minimization, denial, evasion, and diversion, shaming and vilifying, playing the victim or the servant, projection of blame, feigning innocence or confusion, and using anger as a weapon of control.

Another psychologist named Harriet Braiker centered her theory of manipulation almost entirely on the control that manipulators have over their subjects. She identified several ways in which manipulators prey on the weaknesses of their subjects in order to gain and maintain control of them. Those methods include:

1-Using positive reinforcement, such as praise, false sympathy, apologies, and gifts;

2- Using negative reinforcement, such as removing a task or request if only the subject will do what they want;

3- Using intermittent reinforcement, which causes the subject to feel unsure about whether they're doing anything correctly, or what the reward or punishment will be;

4- Causing mental trauma to convey a point, which may scar the subject and bring about anxiety about when and if the trauma will occur again; and

5- Using punishment, including verbal abuse, silent treatment, threats, blackmail, or intimidation.

Exploiting Vulnerability

Both Simon and Braiker agree that a manipulator must first find a weakness in their subject before beginning to employ manipulative tactics. Their combined inventory of emotional vulnerabilities is a veritable laundry list of the softer side of humanity. These vulnerabilities are:

1- Lack of assertiveness or the ability to stand up for themselves;

2- Being too eager to please others or being emotionally dependent on others;

3- Low self-esteem or the belief that they deserve to be treated in a manipulative manner;

4- Naivete or willingness to give their manipulator the benefit of the doubt, being a Pollyanna about the capabilities of others;

5- A lack of a strong sense of self.

Renowned psychiatrist Martin Kantor offers even more traits which make a person susceptible to becoming the subject of a manipulator. According to

Kantor, not only are these people naïve, dependent, and lacking in self-esteem, they may also be narcissistic, craving the attention from the manipulator. Also, people who are vulnerable to manipulation may be materialistic, greedy, or masochistic. People who are lonely, elderly, and altruistic may also fall prey to a manipulator, as well as those who are impressionable and/or impulsive.

Why Use Manipulation?

People who use manipulation do so because they feel there is something to gain from their actions. There are several reasons why people do this, but much of it comes down to the need for power or control. There are some that use manipulation for the purpose of defrauding others, such as the many elder scams we hear about these days, and there's always the classic Nigerian prince email- send them a thousand dollars so they can send you a million! This seems too good to be true because it is. Some people use manipulation as a game, to see if they can control others, but for their own amusement, not to achieve a particular goal.

Some manipulation stems from true sociopathy, psychopathy, and other personality disorders. In these cases, especially socio- and psychopathy, the perpetrators of the manipulation are incapable of feeling empathy for others and see people as tools to be used in their game of life. They may not even be trying to hurt people, but don't know how to treat them as human beings, and therefore feel nothing when others get hurt.

Real-life Scenarios to Help You Understand Using Manipulation

Manipulation occurs every day, all around us. If we choose to be a manipulator, how can we be sure to do it effectively? Let's say you want your girlfriend to move in with you, but she's resisting because she likes the freedom of living alone. You could try a persuasion argument, but if that doesn't work, what's your next step?

You could undermine her sense of independence, but beginning to point out that one time she burned a meal and almost started a fire. Is she sure she should be living alone? You could also remind her that she needs someone to make sure she gets up for work on time because she's a heavy sleeper that sometimes misses alarms. By planting the seeds of doubt in her mind, she will begin to question her own capabilities and will come to the conclusion that she needs to live with you.

To be an effective manipulator, much like being an effective persuader, you need to know your audience. Prey on the insecurities of your subject to open their minds up to doubt. Remember, the goal of manipulation is to change your subject's perception of reality.

Don't Want to Be Manipulated?

No one wants to feel that they've fallen victim to a manipulator. It's a sinking sensation that causes self-doubt and self-loathing. It's happened to everyone- you find out a friend wasn't really a friend, you have a romantic relationship go sour, or you have an issue with a coworker that wasn't quite on the level. How can you learn to recognize the signs of manipulation before you get hurt?

There always warning signs or red flags when it comes to manipulation. Being aware of and being able to spot these signs will help you avoid the use of psychological manipulation against you. If you feel you are being manipulated, take time to look for these signs:

1- Denial of truth, especially in regard to promises made or insults hurled;

2- Use of guilt or blame, by turning everything into someone else's fault;

3- Use of anger or threats, against you or others;

4- Use of belittlement towards you for minor 'infractions';

5- Testing of limits, to see how far you can be pushed before becoming emotional;

6- Convincing you to give up something you love, like a possession or a hobby; and

7- Lying or cheating to get something they want, regardless of the cost to others.

If you can be aware enough to see these warning signs, you may be able to remove yourself from the situation or relationship before the damage is done. It's important to remind yourself that you are not deserving of manipulation and that you've done nothing to provoke it. You are not someone else's puppet or pet- be yourself and find the strength to stand up to your manipulator.

Chapter 9: The Art Of Persuasion

We are moving into more depth on how you can use psychology to help your internal growth and to aid you advance your life using the most ethical practices. The first psychologically sound method that will not only help you do that but also fend off dark psychology users and manipulators is called the art of persuasion.

The art of persuasion is the methodology of getting people to see things in the way that you do so they act in a certain way to benefit both parties. Simply telling someone to do something and having them do it is not persuasion. An example of this is telling a child to go to sleep at a certain hour every night. While the child will comply because of his or her respect for a parent or guardian's authority, the child has not been persuaded to go to sleep at that time. Without the parent or guardian's exertion of authority, the child would not go to bed at that time. The child's belief that this bed time is in his or best interest has not been changed.

Likewise, carrying out a boss's orders or doing an assignment deemed necessary by a professor is not persuasion. Buying a brand-named item because it is on sale does not count as persuasion either as the buyer will resort to his or her normal buying practices once prices return to normal.

None of the scenarios outlined above count as persuasion because the person who does the action has not changed his or her belief due to the influence of the authoritative party.

Persuasion requires that a person act in a certain way because of that change in belief. Therefore, persuasion is accomplished when there is an accompanying change in attitude with action.

The concept of persuasion is easy – get other people to see things the way that you do and then act on that belief. The methodology is difficult, however. This difficulty lies in the fact that a person needs to tap into another person's core belief system to make that change in attitude that leads to action. Luckily, there is a system for practicing the art of persuasion that anyone can learn and implement. These techniques will be discussed below.

Is Persuasion Ethical?

Persuasion is not manipulation. The use of manipulation is intended to coerce someone else into doing something that is not in their best interests. Persuasion, on the other hand, works by getting people to do things that are not only in their best interest but also in the benefit of the persuader.

Like any other expression of art, persuasion on its own is neither good nor bad. The question of morality or immorality only arises due to how it is used. If a person uses persuasion to harm and manipulate then of course, this person has used the art in a way that is deemed unethical. There are, of course, many instances where the art of persuasion has been used unethically. In such cases, the persuader only had their interests at heart and was not concerned with that of other people. One of the principles of the art of persuasion (discussed below) is that the person being persuaded must gain value or be better off from being persuaded, when persuasion is being done in an ethical manner.

A dark psychology user does not adhere to this principle and can even perpetrate a crime by persuading someone in a manner that is harmful to that party. This is termed undue influence and occurs when a dark psychology user or manipulator uses persuasion techniques to persuade a person to act in a way that contrary to their free will or has dire consequences for that person. An example of this is a caretaker that persuades an incapacitated person to change the terms of their will so that the caretaker receives all of their possessions. From this example, you can see that undue influence occurs when the persuaded is not in the right frame of mind to make decisions on their own.

Despite the fact that the art of persuasion can be used in a negative way, there is a lot of good that can come out of the art. In fact, I bet to say that without the ability to practice this art, a person will find it very difficult to live the life that they want to because success in many areas is dependent on our ability to persuade other people to help us. A person will not get their dream job if they cannot persuade the hiring staff to take them onboard. A person will not marry the one of their dreams if they cannot persuade that person to join them in holy matrimony. At times, a person will not be able to buy their dream home if they cannot persuade the loan officer at the bank to give them a mortgage.

Understanding the art of persuasion also makes it less likely that you will fall victim to someone who uses persuasion in a malicious way. You make yourself less vulnerable to being deceived when you are able to recognize when someone is trying to exert influence over your decision-making. Of course, someone trying to exert influence over your decision-making does not necessarily have to be meant in a malicious way. However, knowing that you have the choice at the end of the day to say yes or no allows you to be in a power position.

In addition to lessening the likelihood that you will be deceived, understanding that art of persuasion also helps improve your social skills and aids in building self-esteem as it increases self-confidence. Practicing the act of persuasion even helps with the management of mental health diseases such as depression and anxiety.

The Principles of Persuasion

Some people are naturally persuasive while it takes some work for other people to get the hang of it. No matter the ease with which a person practices the art of persuasion, there are principles that must be abided by for persuasion to not only be effective but also ethical. We will take a look at each of the principles on which the art of ethical persuasion is founded below.

Reciprocation

The first principle is called reciprocation because it is based off the psychology that when you do for others, they feel compelled to return the favor even without active compulsion by you. For example, if someone gets you a gift you a birthday present, you feel compelled to reciprocate the gesture and give that person something for their birthday. If you are invited out by a friend, you now feel the obligation to invite that friend the next time you are going out to something that is relevant to that person. Reciprocation even extends to social media in this day and age. If someone likes and shares your post on Facebook, you will likely feel the need to extend the same action when that person shares a post.

It is speculated that this is part of human evolution, developed in an effort to help each other survive in the wild. As part of your persuasion technique, start by providing small gestures that help other people. Make it a habit to do this for people in your community, family and workplace. People can often sense when someone is offering a gesture of consideration just to get something back. Therefore, make it part of your regular routine to give to other people. You can do this by volunteering, participating in charity or finding a cause to back.

By doing this, you build a reputation of helping other people. Word spreads quickly and all the target of your persuasion has to do is research a little to find out that your past is indicative of you being a natural giver. This makes you a more trustworthy individual in most people's eyes and therefore, your circle of influence extends. This makes the job of persuasion all the easier.

As a side note, I want to state that considering others and giving back to your community incites great feelings of meaningfulness and accomplishment in a person's life. This is a great way to not only extend your circle of influence but to also derive your purpose in your life.

Commitment

Getting the target of your persuasion to verbally commit to following through with the action that you would desire makes it more likely that follow through will be done. Without that agreement to a course of action by the end of a meeting, that person is less likely to follow through because they have not even a commitment to do so. People typically have an internal pull that makes them want to commit the action that we have previously agreed to. Also, people feel that they are more trustworthy when they follow through with the action that they have committed to. Both of these conditions make it more likely that the act of persuasion will be successful.

Authority

This is a powerful principle in the sphere of persuasion but with its power comes a lot of corruption when in the hands of dark psychology users and manipulators. People tend to go through extreme measures to appease people that they perceive as having an authoritative position over them. For example, many people do not question the actions that their doctor recommended. If that doctor is a dark personality, there is no telling the harm a person can do to themselves in their need to obey someone that they perceive as having authority to dictate their actions.

Many people who wear uniforms such as policemen and nurses are perceived as having a position of authority and therefore, their influence on other people are greater. You can use that to your advantage in an ethical manner.

Even without uniform, a person who is generally take-charge in demeanor can speak of having authority and thus, be more persuasive.

Social Validation

Generally, people are more likely to be persuaded when they have seen proof that an idea works out successfully for other people. Therefore, when trying to persuade other people, ensure that you have gathered social proof that your idea has improved the lives of other people by creating value. We see proof of this every day on social media. Companies and public profiles that have a huge following are more likely to persuade other persons to join that following and to test out products if they are being sold.

Scarcity

Value is a relative scale. Something one person might perceive as highly valuable might be perceived to have low value in the eyes of someone else. For example, one person might perceive a gold chain as highly valuable compared to making connections with their family while another person might perceive interpersonal connections as more valuable than material possessions like a gold chain. However, no matter what the person perceives as valuable, this value is typically perceived in relation to the things that other people want.

I am sure that you have heard them saying that people want what they cannot have and if you are the one providing that thing that is scarce, the job of persuasion becomes all the easier. For example, the person who perceives a gold chain as being more valuable than interpersonal connections may not have easy access to materials such as these. This item is scarce in that person's life and therefore, more likely to be something that they can be persuaded to obtain if the means is available.

On the other hand, persons who perceives interpersonal connections as more valuable may have a harder time developing those connections or may have went through an experience that shows them that these connections are more valuable than material possessions. Your job as the persuader is to make your target realize that the object of desire is scarce and therefore, valuable. The more value that you bring to the table, even if it is in the form of yourself, the easier it is to convince other people that the point that you are trying to bring across them is valuable.

Likeability

Being liked is a great influencer as it speaks to a person being trusted. The logic is that most people who are untrustworthy have displayed symptoms of that dishonesty and thus, are not liked by many people in general. On the hand, if a person displays trustworthy traits then they are more likely to be liked by people in general. If you like someone or have a friendship set up then it is more likely that you will say yes to their persuasion.

Being likable does not mean that you always have to be agreeable. It simply means that you have to develop a sense of diplomacy and be respectful in the manner that you communicate with other people. Likeability is a great influencing factor in races that are dependent on the opinion of others such as presidential elections.

Chapter 10: Using Neuro-Linguistic Programming To "Manipulate" The Mind

Neuro-linguistic programming is a method for changing somebody's considerations and practices to help accomplish wanted results for them.

The notoriety of neuro-semantic programming or NLP has turned out to be across the board since it began during the 1970s. Its uses incorporate treatment of fears and tension issue and improvement of working environment execution or individual satisfaction.

This article will investigate the hypothesis behind NLP and what proof there is supporting its training.

What is NLP?

NLP utilizes perceptual, conduct, and correspondence strategies to make it simpler for individuals to change their musings and activities.

NLP depends on language preparing yet ought not be mistaken for characteristic language handling, which offers a similar abbreviation.

NLP as a concept was postulated by John Grinder and Bander Richard, who trusted it was conceivable to recognize the examples of contemplations and practices of effective people and to instruct them to other people.

The fluctuating translations of NLP make it difficult to characterize. It is established on the possibility that individuals work by inner "maps" of the world that they learn through tactile encounters.

NLP attempts to identify and adjust oblivious inclinations or confinements of a person's guide of the world.

NLP isn't hypnotherapy. Rather, it works through the cognizant utilization of language to realize changes in somebody's considerations and conduct.

For instance, a focal component of NLP is the possibility that an individual is one-sided towards one tangible framework, known as the favored illustrative framework or PRS.

Advisors can identify this inclination through language. Expressions, for example, "I see your point" may flag a visual PRS. Or on the other hand "I hear your point" may flag a sound-related PRS.

A NLP professional will recognize an individual's PRS and base their restorative structure around it. The system could include affinity building, data social affair, and objective setting with them.

Procedures

NLP is an expansive field of training. All things considered, NLP specialists utilize a wide range of systems that incorporate the accompanying:

• Anchoring: Turning tactile encounters into triggers for certain passionate states.

- Rapport: The specialist tunes into the individual by coordinating their physical practices to improve correspondence and reaction through sympathy.

- Swish example: Changing examples of conduct or thought to go to an ideal rather than an undesired result.

- Visual/sensation separation (VKD): Trying to evacuate negative considerations and sentiments related with a past occasion.

NLP is utilized as a strategy for self-improvement through advancing abilities, for example, self-reflection, certainty, and correspondence.

Specialists have applied NLP monetarily to accomplish work-orientated objectives, for example, improved profitability or employment movement.

All the more broadly, it has been applied as a treatment for mental issue, including fears, misery, summed up tension issue or

GAD, and post-horrible pressure issue or PTSD.

The Validity

Deciding the adequacy of NLP is trying for a few reasons.

NLP has not been dependent upon a similar standard of logical thoroughness as progressively settled treatments, for example, psychological social treatment or CBT.

The absence of formal guideline and NLP's business worth imply that cases of its adequacy can be narrative or provided by a NLP supplier. NLP suppliers will have a monetary enthusiasm for the achievement of NLP, so their proof is hard to utilize.

Besides, logical research on NLP has delivered blended outcomes.

A few examinations have discovered advantages related with NLP. For instance, an investigation distributed in the diary Counseling and Psychotherapy Research discovered psychotherapy patients had improved mental indications and life quality in the wake of having NLP contrasted with a control gathering.

However, an audit distributed in The British Journal of General Practice of 10 accessible investigations on NLP was less positive.

It finished up there was little proof for the viability of NLP in treating wellbeing related conditions, including tension issue, weight the executives, and substance abuse. This was because of the restricted sum and nature of the examination thinks about that were accessible, instead of proof that indicated NLP didn't work out.

However, a further research survey distributed in 2015 found NLP treatment to positively affect people with social or mental issues, and because the creators said more examination was required.

The hypothetical reason for NLP has likewise pulled in analysis for lacking proof based help.

A paper distributed in 2009 reasoned that following three decades, the hypotheses behind NLP were as yet not tenable, and proof for its viability was just recounted.

A 2010 survey paper looked to evaluate the examination discoveries identifying with the speculations behind NLP. Of the 33 included investigations, just 18 percent were found to help NLP's fundamental speculations.

In this way, notwithstanding over 4 many years of its reality, neither the adequacy of NLP or the legitimacy of the speculations have been plainly exhibited by strong research.

Likewise, it is significant, that exploration has for the most part been directed in helpful settings, with few examinations into the viability of NLP in business conditions.

Considering how well NLP functions has a few handy issues too, adding to the absence of lucidity encompassing the subject. For instance, it is hard to straightforwardly think about investigations given the scope of various strategies, methods, and results.

Chapter 11: Sneaky Ways Of Covert Hypnosis

Often done while having what might seem to be a normal conversation, covert hypnosis – by definition – means that a person is being hypnotized without realizing what's going on.

While this might bother or upset some people, it's important to know the facts. The fact is that we were all covertly hypnotized while we were kids and our brains were still forming. Our parents and anyone with any authority over us and our learning experiences did this to us, not knowing that they were actually hypnotizing the children they loved. And we've all done it to our own children and any we have authority over as well.

We put our ideas and expectations into their brains over and over again. If you think about it for a moment, you will understand how this whole thing works. You might've heard your mother say something like, "We are Baptists, and we believe in that religion and that one alone."

You were never given a choice about what religion you were - it was decided for you. But as you grew up, you found yourself truly believing the way you'd been told to.

But many of us began to hear things from others and see things on television that had us questioning things. It was when our brains matured that we used our own mind to make decisions. And as long as you still use your own mind and don't just believe whatever anyone tells you, then you won't fall victim to covert hypnosis.

Conversational Hypnosis

This is by far the most common type of covert hypnosis that anyone will encounter. It's done on all platforms too – social, media, advertising – you name it, this technique has been and is currently being used.

Keywords That Disengage The Conscious Mind

To get a person to stop thinking clearly on their own, some words help the covert hypnotist to shut down the conscious mind. Using words like imagine and relax are just a couple.

Here is a whole list of keywords for you to use or be aware of them being used on you.

Envision.

Visualize.

Picture.

Dream.

See.

Think.

Conceive.

Invent.

Concoct.

Make up.

Dream up.

Make-believe.

Think of.

Suppose.

Expect.

Assume.

Presume.

Guess.

Understand.

Diminish.

Reduce.

Lower.

Ease.

Unwind.

Calm down.

Slow down.

Let go.

Loosen up.

Lighten up.

Settle Down.

Rest.

Take it easy.

Put your feet up.

Chill out.

Lie down.

Loosen.

These words are powerful enough to stop a person from their present train of thought and put them in a state that makes it much easier to get into their minds and warp them in the ways you wish to.

Visualization

Much like a writer who wants to take their readers on a real journey in their minds, words can be used to make you visualize things.

When someone asks you to see something that could be, they are putting a picture into your head, trying to get you to do what they want you to. Seeing is believing after all — even if you're just seeing it in your mind.

Ambiguity

As defined by Wikipedia - ambiguity is a type of meaning in which a phrase, statement or resolution is not explicitly defined, making several interpretations plausible. A common aspect of ambiguity is uncertainty. It is thus an attribute of any idea or statement whose intended meaning cannot be definitively resolved according to a rule or process with a finite number of steps.

If this confuses you, then you are now witnessing ambiguity at its finest — politicians bank on this kind of thing. How man speeches have you listened to that when finished you have no idea what the heck all that talk was all about?

Beware this type of speech as it puts your brain into a semi-conscious state as it tries to find something of interest or importance within all the words that the speaker is spewing or droning on about.

Vagueness

Being vague is what most people do when they have no intention of committing to anything. When someone says maybe – most people take that as a no. When someone says, might – most people take that as a no.

There are various ways of being vague. You can be trying not to tell someone the truth about something. Let's say that Sandra has a new hair cut and you don't care for it. But she asks you if you like it and you're stuck.

"Um, well, it's very different for you, isn't it?" You might vaguely ask.

When someone doesn't answer you outright, they're being vague with you to avoid something. Maybe it's to avoid hurting your feelings. So you might not want to push it and just accept the fact that not everyone is going to agree with everything you do or say.

I'm Not Going To Tell You

I'm sure you've heard someone tell you that they aren't going to tell you something but then they tell it to you right away.

Take this little sentence for example. "I'm not going to tell you to eat more chicken, but research shows that you need to eat more chicken."

This is so in your face, that we sometimes miss the fact that we're being directed to something. When someone acts as if they aren't telling you what to do, that disengages the mind, then they enter what they want you to do to reengage it in the way they want you to.

Think about how many things you've never wanted until someone told you something great about it, after telling you that they aren't going to tell you what to do.

It is truly crazy how our minds work.

Embedded Commands

These simple statements are mixed into about a paragraph worth of words. It's most often used in advertising to get people to make a purchase that they wouldn't otherwise make.

Take this example of embedded commands that will be written in bold so you can spot them.

I won't tell you to **buy my product** because I respect you and believe that you have the right to make your own decisions. What I will do is let you know enough about my product so you can **think about my product**, imagine what it can do for you. And then you can make your own decision to **buy my product**.

You can clearly see how your mind is being taken over. You are expected to buy this product because you are told twice to do it and once to think about it. In the end, you most likely will want to take a chance and buy it since the sales technique seemed not to be too forceful and off-putting.

Cause And Effect

Cause and effect are powerful tools in the mind game business. Some scientists believe that people can see cause and effect even when it doesn't really exist.

If someone tells you that you broke a rule and so you have to be punished – that is cause and effect. But what makes their rule your rule?

Maybe walking on the left side of the road is what they're saying you did that broke a rule that you didn't know they had. And when they tell you that the punishment for breaking that rule is to pay a fine of a hundred dollars, you are startled, stunned, then outraged.

But chances are you will pay the fine and swear never to go back to that place again. You saw cause and effect when it didn't really exist. Because you didn't make sure there really was a rule like that and the conman got your money.

Be sure that you can clearly see that there is a real cause to affect you before you accept it as a fact.

Key Takeaways

Now you can spot things you might not have been able to before.

Conversation hypnosis is the most commonly used form of hypnosis.

Visualization is used to make you see something that's not there or tangible.

Ambiguity is the art of talking in circles that lead to nowhere.

Vagueness is when one skirts around an issue without giving their real opinions or answers.

Telling someone that you won't tell them what to do, then tell them what to do anyway.

Embedding commands to hide the fact that you want to tell someone to do something.

Cause and effect, knowing when there is a real one and a fake one.

Exercises

If someone begins talking to you, using any of the keywords designed to disengage your conscious mind, what will you do to counteract this?

The next time you hear someone say that they aren't going to tell you something then do, what will you do?

If someone tells you that you have to suffer the effect that your actions have caused, what will you do about that?

Are you going to use any of these techniques to try to get others to do what you want them to do? And why or why not?

Chapter 12: Brainwashing

Brainwashing is one of the more aggressive forms of manipulation. It is more commonly used by cults, religious or political leaders, with prisoners of war and in abusive relationships.

Being brainwashed creates confusion about your identity. Feelings of self-doubt are the first signs of being brainwashed, even though we're not always aware of what's happening.

Personality traits such as self-doubt, a weak sense of self, lacking confidence or feeling guilty are enough to make one susceptible to brainwashing. The opposite is also true, a stronger sense of self and emotional stability makes us more resistant to such techniques. So not everyone is a good candidate for brainwashing. Certain techniques which are taught to soldiers can help prevent them from being brainwashed. These include using visualizations, repetition of mantras and other related meditation methods. Also having knowledge as to exactly how brainwashing works (Lifton's theory described later in this chapter) helps strengthen the psyche against such an attack.

It's not only others who brainwash us, we sometimes do it to ourselves by blindly accepting everything we hear and read. If for instance, you start associating with negative people or living in an environment which instills feelings of fear or self-doubt, you may undergo a subtle change in personality and character. On the flip-side people suffering from low self-esteem or confidence, can 'brainwash' themselves through affirmations, meditations, reading and learning how to become the people they would most like to be – confident, charming, successful or whatever. Through constant reinforcement and repetition of either positive or negative stimulus, we change as a result.

It is often said in self-help circles that the people we surround ourselves with mirror back to us who we are likely to become in the future. Surround yourself with happy, successful people and you'll be more likely to become happy and successful. Surround yourself with negative people and you will also become more like them.

Signs you're being brainwashed

Signs of being brainwashed vary from intense and dangerous brainwashing by cult leaders or psychopaths to everyday subliminal influencing we endure from our families, employers, the Government, commercials, culture and social media.

If we're constantly fed similar information through repetition, day after day, month after month and year after year, you eventually start becoming it, no matter how ludicrous it might be. Brainwashing happens every day to young children. How children are programmed from a young age is effectively brainwashing. When the personality has not yet fully formed it is highly impressionable.

If you were fortunate enough to have been brought up by a loving, positive and supportive family, you will have probably developed adequate defense mechanisms by the time you reach adolescence. However, if your parenting was not predominantly positive, it likely filled your mind with negative and self-limiting beliefs.

Character-development can be a long difficult process and without sufficient self-esteem instilled in the earlier part of life, we're unlikely to develop the confidence we will need later in life. But it's hard to develop self-esteem if we're repeatedly told whilst growing up, 'I don't think you'll ever amount to much', or 'You're good for nothing', or 'I don't think you have it in you to succeed', such statements may not have been passed with much conviction, but they tend to stay with us and color how we perceive the world and ourselves. Although parents usually mean well, they sometimes do damage, especially if they believe they're encouraging us to work harder by hinting that we're stupid, or that everybody else is smarter or better behaved. All though reverse psychology can work, its usually not helpful for young developing minds.

Our culture brainwashes us into believing that we are not pretty enough, smart enough or good enough for what we want in life. After years of being told such things, we start unconsciously believing them, even though our ego may reject the suggestion as unfair or wrong, these limiting beliefs run in the background of our programming.

Many of us go through life afraid of going for what our heart desires because from a young age we have been brainwashed into believing we're not good enough or deserving of what we truly want.

Systematic Breakdown of Brainwashing

In psychological domains, brainwashing is known as 'thought reforming', which is closely related to social influence, in which we are being influenced by society and our environment constantly.

Brainwashing is comprised of 3 different methods of mind control which is why it's so effective. Firstly, it involves the 'compliance' technique, this looks to change someone's behavior but is not concerned with the subject's current beliefs, it's the 'just do it' attitude. The second method used is Persuasion, 'do it because you'll gain something - feel happier, more positive, healthy, successful'. The third and final method is education, this is also known as the 'propaganda method' - where we are taught things we don't necessarily believe in. This method is also the most like brainwashing as it tries to change a person's understanding and beliefs. The underlying rule here is, 'do it because it's the right thing to do'.

Brainwashing is comprised of these three aspects, which when used coherently makes it a powerful form of influence that eventually overrides a person's will.

Since brainwashing is such an extreme form of mind control, it requires certain pre-requisites for it to be successful. Some of the key elements needed include complete isolation and absolute dependency from the subject, this is why it tends to happen more in isolated situations such as prisons and cults for example. For brainwashing to be successful the manipulator must have complete control over the victim. This includes controlling their sleep patterns, meal times, use of bathroom and any other fulfillment of basic human needs. Through such a heavy dependency, the target's identity eventually breaks, to the point they don't know who they are anymore. At this moment, they can be 'brainwashed' with a new set of ideas, beliefs, attitudes, and behaviors.

So, brainwashing is possible under the specific conditions mentioned, but at the same time, it's difficult for this to occur in everyday life. Also, the effects of brainwashing are usually not long-term because the victim's true self and original identity can never be completely erased but can be hidden or repressed for a short amount of time. Once the 'new identity' stops being enforced the victim's original thoughts and beliefs gradually begin to resurface.

In the 1950's, an American psychologist Robert Jay Lifton studied the effects the Korean war and Chinese camps had on its prisoners. A number of American soldiers had been captured during the Korean way and brainwashed. He uncovered the specific steps which were undertaken to break the prisoners down and open them up to be brainwashed. These processes began by breaking down the prisoners 'sense of self' which would eventually lead to a change in attitude and beliefs. Using Lifton's school of thought, we can break down brainwashing into main three sections.

1. Breaking down of the original self

2. Introducing a possibility of Salvation

3. Rebuilding the Self

With the basic structure in place. Lifton further broke down the brainwashing process into 10 individual stages (A-J) -

A. Assault on Identity

B. Guilt

C. Self-Betrayal

D. Breaking Point

E. Leniency

F. Compulsion to confess

G. Channeling of guilt

H. Releasing guilt

I. Progress and Harmony

J. Final Confession & Rebirth

Every one of these stages is carried out in complete isolation, which means normal social and environmental reference points are absent. These initial influencers are enhanced by 'mind-clouding' methods such as hunger and sleep deprivation - both of which make the target considerably weaker. This is further compounded by a constant threat of violence or harm. All these factors prevent the victim from being able to think independently and critically.

1. Breaking down of the original self

This comprises of sections A-D of the ten stages of brainwashing.

A. Assault on Identity

The brainwashing process begins with attacks on the target's sense of self (ego/identity) – When we're not being ourselves, our core belief system is disrupted. The brainwasher will deny the victim of everything he thinks he is i.e. 'you're not a soldier', 'you're not American' etc. This can continue for weeks or even months, to the point the target is left incredibly disorientated, confused and fatigued. Gradually, his beliefs about himself begin to weaken.

B. Guilt

As the identity crisis is beginning to take root, the target is made to feel a crushing sense of guilt that he is bad. He is continuously targeted for any minor things and attacked for the sins he has committed. This can include everything from his beliefs about himself to the way he eats or drinks. By increasing the feelings of guilt and shame, he feels that everything he does is wrong or bad.

C. Self-Betrayal

As the victim is wallowing in self-guilt and shame, he is forced or threatened into dis-identifying from his family, friends, country, peers or anyone who holds the same 'bad' belief systems as him. Such a betrayal of his own values and of those he feels some loyalty towards increases the feelings of shame while further losing touch with his identity.

D. Breaking Point

At this stage, the target is 'broken' and begins to question himself. He doesn't know who he is anymore and asks, 'Who am I and what am I supposed to do?' With the impact of the identity breakdown, feelings of deep shame and unworthiness increase. Along with betraying his long-standing beliefs, the victim goes through a 'nervous breakdown' - which includes depression, emotional suffering, and disorientation. The target at this point will feel completely alone and be incredibly vulnerable as he's lost all understanding of himself. Here the manipulator introduces a new belief system as a reprise to prevent the suffering.

2. Introducing possibility of Salvation

The brainwashing process now moves into the second of the three stages.

E. Leniency

The victim is offered help and support. With the target in such a compromised state, they are presented with a small act of kindness or relief from the constant abuse. This may be in the shape of food or via an emotional connection. For instance, the manipulator may ask the victim personal questions about his life and interests. In the wake of long psychological suffering, any small act of kindness can seem huge. This makes the victim feel a sense of gratitude and relief which is disproportionate to the offering, he may almost feel like he's been 'saved'.

F. Compulsion to confess

For the first time, the target feels a sense of relief from the constant assault on him and his character. In response to this, he feels compelled to reciprocate the acts of kindness he has received by possibly confessing his part in the war. This will help him to feel further relief from the guilt and shame which he has been feeling.

G. Channeling of guilt

After prolonged periods of pain, confusion, breakdowns with brief moments of reprieve the victim's sense of guilt has lost meaning. He now doesn't know what he has done wrong, he just feels himself to be wrong. This makes the target a clean slate, which opens the door for the manipulator to begin influencing him. He can 'channel' the victim's guilt into any areas or subjects as he decides. He will relate the victim's guilt to his beliefs, such as the country he serves, which is why he feels bad. The contrast between the old painful beliefs and new (relieving) beliefs is established. The old is linked to pain and psychological disturbance whereas the new is associated with the possibility of relief and no pain. This is an NLP technique which helps create new 'neuro-associations' within the mind.

H. Releasing guilt

The victim comes to understand that it's not himself who is guilty or shameful but in fact his beliefs. These are the cause of the bad painful feelings he feels. So, he begins to believe he can escape the pain by dis-identifying from the old beliefs. All it requires is that he denounces everything he thought he was associated with (his old belief system) and the pain will be relieved. At this point, the victim will confess even more. With these confessions, he is also releasing the old belief system and as a result, is pushing his old identity further away.

3. Rebuilding the Self

I. Progress and Harmony

The victim feels he now has a choice. He is introduced to a new way of thinking, which is shown as the 'right' way. At this point, the abuse has come to a halt. Instead, the target is offered comfort and suffers less psychological disturbances, which makes him neurologically associate the relief with the new 'good' belief system. Like classic manipulation tactics, the victim feels like he has the freedom of choice to decide between the old set of beliefs or the new ones presented to him. Since the target has already dis-identified from his old beliefs in response to leniency, by making his choice to choose the 'new' belief system he releases his feelings of guilt further. His new identity and sense of self-feels safer since it's nothing like the old one which led to his breakdown.

J. Final Confession & Rebirth

At the final stage, the victim is 'converted' and feels a sense of rebirth. He may declare he has chosen 'good' over evil. With the contrasting difference of the painful old ways, with the relief of the new, he hangs to his new identity as though it saved his life. He rejects his old belief system and even turns against it. To close the process there maybe rituals and ceremonies carried out by the manipulators to welcome the target into his new community.

This detailed description of the brainwashing process was created by Lifton after his study of war prisoners from the Korean War.

Brainwashing Techniques

As we now understand, brainwashing doesn't occur overnight but is usually a series of actions taken simultaneously over a period of time, which eventually results into a changed personality. Perception and behavior change, sometimes to such an extent that the victim becomes unrecognizable to their friends or peers.

The techniques used and the speed with which the personality changes depends on many things, but most of all on whether the target is being subjected to brainwashing against their will (in which case they'll naturally resist as much as they can) or whether they don't know they're being brainwashed (e.g. in cults) and believe all the ideas being impressed upon them are their own and that they themselves are making the decisions. This could be deemed successful brainwashing, as the victim is unaware of what's occurring.

Most common overt and covert brainwashing techniques:

➤ Repetition and nagging

It's hard not to start believing something or at least begin doubting one's self if someone is constantly repeating the same thing over and over every day, for months or even years.

➢ Isolation

It is easier to control someone if they have no access to sources of information which conflict with the brainwashing material. If the target talks to someone about the ideas being imposed upon them and other people understand what's happening, they may scupper the chances for a successful brainwash. This tactic is often witnessed in abusive relationships, where one partner doesn't want the other to communicate with friends or family incase their motives are uncovered.

➢ Blind obedience

This prevents the victim from thinking for themselves.

➢ Responsibility

One central brainwashing technique is to make someone feel responsible for their faults and the things that go wrong in their life. If they make mistakes, do something poorly, or if things don't go according to plan, making them feel responsible leaves them feeling negative emotions such as guilt and shame, which lowers their defenses and opens them up for manipulation.

➤ Guilt and fear

These are used extensively as part of an overall emotional manipulation plan. When a huge guilt complex is imposed, we start believing we're deserving of any resulting punishment.

➤ Love bombing

Some cults shower new members with love and attention to make them feel special and part of their 'family'. These childish games cause age regression and encourage obedience.

➤ My way is the right way attitude

No questions or criticism of leadership is allowed. When everyone is obedient, the group is easier to control - Group think.

➤ Repetitive, mind-dumbing practices

Chanting, singing, dancing and body therapies all reduce critical thinking. Research shows our brain can only focus on one thing at a time, so a great way to slow down the thinking process (which may lead to questioning) is by engaging in repetitive chants or similar activities.

The aim of these techniques is to prompt the target into accepting new ideas blindly, without questioning. For that to happen, the mind has to become dormant – hypnotized, drugged or made helpless, powerless or childlike.

As Mokokoma Mokhonoana once said, 'Most people do not have a problem with you thinking for yourself, as long as your conclusions are the same as or at least compatible with their beliefs.'

Brainwashing yourself into positive thinking

Although brainwashing is deemed a negative practice and is generally associated with mental abuse it can also be used for positive purposes by helping us overcome bad habits, insecurities or low self-esteem and confidence. By simply applying various brainwashing techniques we can positively impact our psychology.

Self-brainwashing can be used as a form of self-help therapy of replacing old, outdated thought patterns with new healthier programs which can help us get more out of life.

The key word here is BELIEF. Just as the famous Law of Attraction states - you get what you think you'll get! With self-brainwashing, if you convince yourself you can do something, you'll eventually develop the courage to do so. But if you believe you can't, you will likely be right also.

4 Self-brainwashing techniques:

— Identify a negative thought pattern

Identify a negative thought or belief that's been holding you back. How long have you felt this way? Can you connect the programming to any early life experiences? Are you aware of how this belief has affected your life? What do you think your life would have been like if it weren't for this negative thought pattern? Do you believe you are what others tell you? What skills or abilities do you wish you had?

– Acknowledging the damage

Be aware of any negative emotional, mental or physical harm this thought pattern has done to you, then make the decision to do something about it. Negative programming can be reversed, but it takes time, so be prepared to work on this issue for a long time if need be.

– The Power of Suggestion

Much of our negative thinking comes from suggestions we take in from others. Think of how many times someone has spoken to you negatively, said you were fat, stupid or unintelligent? Eventually, when these suggestions are heard repeatedly they tend to became our reality.

We can reverse such damage by purposefully taking our suggestions onto a more positive path by consciously choosing positive beliefs. Whatever flaws you believe you have, they can often be reversed. One such way is to constantly tell yourself what you'd like to become, by verbally affirming (or thinking) how successful, healthy or confident you are. Eventually, with commitment, these suggestions can come true as our actions and behaviors gradually begin to follow the constant positive reinforcement we're feeding ourselves.

– **Repetition**

Repetition is successfully used in self-brainwashing. Consistently reinforce positive thoughts about yourself or your self-image by repeating confidence-boosting words and affirmations throughout the day. If it helps, use sticky notes on your desk, inside your car, on the fridge, and other places where you'll often see them. Or, try chanting short phrases such as, 'I am smart', 'I am successful', 'People like me' or whatever you're trying to change.

Alternatively, you can make it a daily habit to rewrite your chosen affirmations over and over in a notebook or journal. Constantly seeing and hearing the same ideas eventually results in constant belief in them as they are accepted and integrated by the subconscious.

We can take this further by reading books associated with the skills we want to develop, listening to audiobooks or watching Youtube videos about the related topic. With a constant bombardment from various modalities, we begin to influence and change our psychology.

Chapter 13: Brainwashing And Other Mind Control Tactics

The first documented use of the word "brainwashing" happened in the 1950s during the Korean War and was soon made popular as the ideology promoted terror, anxiety and many other destructive emotions among individuals of all cultures, creeds and sects around the world. It was used to define the method of manipulation used by Korean and Chinese soldiers to influence the mental state of American prisoners of war under their authority. During their stay in foreign concentration camps, POWs were exposed to several brainwashing methods (most of them novel and previously untested) until they denied their identities, switched national allegiance against their country of origin, and even confessed to war crimes in which they had played no part. Since its inception and general recognition as psychological development, brainwashing has been a point of reference for many people; from those who want to use it, those who want to reclaim ownership of themselves and those who want to prevent ever having to deal with a form of brainwashing or with other methods and intentions. While the word and its research may be newer in the field of psychology, the basic mechanisms and techniques used in brainwashing have been around for as long as humans have tried to influence the way others think, act and respond. In this book, we are going to look deeper at brainwashing, the fundamentals of brainwashing, and how to prevent it from becoming a weapon used against you, particularly by those who plan to cause damage.

BRAINWASHING IS DIFFERENT FROM OTHER MIND CONTROL METHODS

Brainwashing is not a novel phenomenon in psychology or even in human history when you look at the components of the technique and where they have evolved. It is sometimes referred to as "thought reform" by those who research it critically; the term of the technique was provided thanks to the description of the process of brainwashing. It is described as the deliberate act of altering the thoughts or emotions of another individual or group of persons against their will (and often without their awareness). Brainwashing methods are used wherever you look, and not always for deceitful or harmful purposes. Some methods are used regularly in advertising firms or for political campaigns. Like persuasion and manipulation, it is hard to recognize until you are fully submerged into it. However, unlike those two techniques that also have deep connections in psychology and Dark Psychology, brainwashing is less efficient unless it is extended to large groups of potential targets (like cults and political supporters).

Here is a quick comparison of techniques to make it easier for those unfamiliar with the field of Dark Psychology to discern the difference:

I. Persuasion, when utilized, is meant to compel the subject to believe that they have modified their own minds by deliberate thinking and enhanced awareness of the situation. People who use this approach want their targets to have a shift of perspective that makes them feel good about their choice to improve their thought or actions. They want to control their future without changing their history.

II. Manipulation is the effective transformation of one's thoughts and emotions by forceful coercion as a means of gaining influence over one's actions for a greedy and often malicious reason. The manipulator has no concern for the history or long-term future of their target except what they need to understand to achieve control over them for their advantage.

III. Brainwashing techniques are in the middle of the two. They are not always used with malicious intent, although the term has gained that notoriety because of its success with those who want to use it as a means of control or dominance over others. The main objective of brainwashing is for the brainwasher (sometimes referred to as the agent) to cause the subject to adjust their thoughts and emotions to comply with their fundamental values and previous experiences in order to obtain influence over how they think and behave. When used for false or immoral purposes, the main aim of brainwashing is to attack a person at their very core (their perception of who they are, their values and ethical views) and to force them to question themselves so that they accept the new "truths" they have been subjected to as fact, giving them reassurance or affirmation when they seek to stabilize their life.

More subtle forms of brainwashing have been efficiently used to sell products such as tobacco by putting subliminal messages in videos, television shows, magazines, radio and other outlets. They may not be ads specifically for the product but simply images of people using and consuming cigarettes as they go about their everyday lives. Some of the brainwashing techniques popularized through this kind of marketing advertisement involved subtle but effective elements including making sure that the person with the cigarette in the video or photo is always happy and joking, or choosing the right colors and symbols to lure customers in and make them want to go straight to the supermarket to pick up a pack.

STEPS FOR SUCCESSFUL BRAINWASHING

Individual strategies do not have an important impact when it comes to trying to brainwash others. Brainwashing is a process that involves a carefully selected set of methods that are formulated based on the target, purpose and time the agent has to accomplish the ultimate goal or brainwashing method. Irrespective of the specifics, the fundamental forms of brainwashing are consistent for those that are studying, exercising and mastering their strategies.

I. Rewrite the Past: The first step is the most important when it comes to effective brainwashing. Rewriting a person's life starts by having them doubt their convictions, their background and anything else they have experienced and hold sacred. If the brainwashing agent is unable to make their audience reconsider what they believe, then there is no way they will be able (subconsciously or forcefully) to introduce new information and convictions. Once someone starts to question themselves, they are more likely to become open to new ideas, start seeking answers in their unknown environments, and develop an ambiguous view of the world.

II. Inspire Guilt: Guilt is an effective emotion that brainwashing agents utilize to further coerce their victims to alter their perceptions, feelings and behavioral patterns. By the end of the first phase, the victim is to dismiss whatever they have ever learned or believed (assuming brainwashing is going to plan) and begin to express the fresh thoughts and concepts that their agent wants them to accept. They may be hesitant to continue to embrace new world views or to alter their behaviors completely, but as soon as they not only denounce their previous beliefs but feel bad about them, they become less antagonistic and more responsive to subsequent thought and perception manipulation.

III. The All is Lost Moment: This is a common phenomenon among storytellers and authors who want to build a moment of vulnerability for their protagonists to overcome. The "All is Lost Moment" occurs when a person is forced to the point of despair concerning:

a)   Who they are, their character, and their perception of the world.

b)   Where they have been and what they have done to become the person they are now (the individual they question and have completely lost faith in).

c) What they want for the future, and how they see themselves going there, if at all.

Some of the dangers of brainwashing to the point of despair are the high possibility of suicide by the victim or the possibility that they will harm others after losing interest in human life.

IV. Reaching Out and Making an Offer: Brainwashing is a very lonely method for the victim, even though they may be part of a group. Once they have been psychologically broken down to the point of despair (certainly at this level in any effective brainwashing effort), it provides an opportunity for the agent to establish an emotional bond, shallow or not, to gain their confidence and enable the final transition from their existing psychological state to the mode of thinking or acting that the agent desires. This primary connection can be achieved with something as easy as getting them a drink of fresh water, an additional portion of food or something else that they like. This shows (however disguised) sympathy for the victim and makes them more open to dialogue or engagement. A small act of kindness or a compassionate moment transforms an individual from an enemy to a possible ally.

V. Confession and Desire to Get Involved: To find a way out or improve a situation, people will consider anything that will help them feel happier and reassure them that they are making the right decisions. At this point, the victim is completely under the influence of the agent with little possibility of breaking out before the scheme comes to an end and escaping the repercussions that follow. They may still have suspicions that they are being manipulated, but they are much more susceptible to persuasion and other brainwashing methods if the mechanism is strengthened.

VI. Acceptance and Rebirth: In this final phase, the subject fully accepts the brainwashing cycle, follows the new realities they have been presented with and becomes the new person they have been programmed to be through meticulous training, coaching, manipulating and sometimes even physical abuse (not necessarily brainwashing methods, but often used in political, military, criminal and other darker purposes).

Once all these procedures have been implemented to their fullest extent (or their most effective, depending on the circumstances), the brainwashing phase can be deemed successful, and the agent may have a look at the list of methods that have been used to see how efficient they have been. Psychological research has found that brainwashing is one of the least effective forms of mental and emotional control in which individuals should invest their time because it is so complicated, and the actual results of all the various techniques have yet to be thoroughly explored. The main question that researchers have been asking regarding brainwashing methods from the onset is whether it is as effective as a manipulation tool as people think it is (worry or assume it is) because of the brainwashing mechanism itself or because of the vulnerability of individual targets to psychological control. From there, they ask questions such as: what makes certain individuals more vulnerable than others? Can existing brainwashing strategies be used across genders, ethnicities and social groups to the same effect as others, or can those factors and methods be lost in translation?

POPULAR BRAINWASHING STRATEGIES USED IN GENERAL AND DARK PSYCHOLOGY

One brainwashing strategy often seen in different industries and contexts is a continued reinforcement of the idea or conviction that they want the victim to accept. This can be achieved by auditory methods, such as listening to a repetitive soundtrack; by verbal means, such as pressuring the victim to repeat a sentence over and over until that is all they can talk of; or visually by inserting it in a video clip that is then repeated continually as the only light source or sound in the victim's containment area. Another method involves having a person surrender their logical thinking mechanism and focus on their emotional impulses to decide their choices, perceptions and behavior. Emotional reactions can be motivated by several factors such as defensiveness from fear of exclusion, or violent outbursts due to the target being so irritated or frustrated by the agent that they hit out rather than taking a deep breath and carefully considering any action or request. One of the ways agents may achieve this is by taking the time to continually confuse their target by giving them snippets of information (which may or may not be true) just to the point where they will be interested. This withholding of details helps keep the target returning to them to find out more; to feel as though they are expanding their understanding of the world. It leaves them more susceptible to manipulation when the agent is ready to initiate the brainwashing cycle in full force.

Emotional control and coercion are basic methods of brainwashing, mainly once the agent has already acquired the confidence of their target and is ready to move ahead with their strategy. This technique involves modifying the emotional condition of their target either by causing anxiety or by stimulating the recollection of traumatic events until the target is so emotionally exhausted that they are unable to recognize that they are being manipulated or even realize that something is wrong. Skilled brainwashing agents find a way to make their target feel reassured by their presence or eagerness to sit down and pay attention to their emotional problems, particularly if the target is someone who does not readily reveal themselves and their feelings to others.

CONSEQUENCES OF BRAINWASHING ON INDIVIDUALS AND GROUPS

The consequences of brainwashing itself (and how powerful it is as a form of psychological manipulation) have been questioned by various groups of scholars and analysts who have spent years studying American soldiers who, on their return to the United States after being liberated from war camps, were identified as victims of brainwashing. They believed that those they spoke to were most likely influenced through physical torture and negligence, and not by the real brainwashing methods. A primary reason for believing this is that, out of the hundreds of thousands of inmates who have have been through brainwashing trials, fewer than two dozen have experienced any progress. Nevertheless, that number just takes into account the troops who chose to return to the United States and not those who were so hardened against their home country that they decided to stay in the land of their abductors even after the war ended and they were all freed.

Cults around the globe have played a significant role in brainwashing and its impacts with their persistent involvement. From the outside, it is safe to suggest that cults are strange and it is hard to comprehend why anyone would want to get actively engaged. However, brainwashing, coercion and other powerful methods of psychological domination are widely used by the members or recruiters of these organizations, and they are some of the most studied and well-tested agents and manipulators of human society. The primary way they achieve their goals is by exploiting those who are most susceptible to manipulation, making them feel special and part of a group, and then influencing them by deceptive empathy or persuasion that what they do or advocate for is sincerely righteous and honorable.

Efficient brainwashing can have several long-term effects on individuals and groups of people. Some of the most popular side effects that can be relieved or eliminated through an anti-brainwashing procedure (more commonly known as deprogramming) include:

I. Crushed Sense of Confidence: This can often contribute to a sequence of difficult and destructive actions, such as dependency on alcohol or the use of powerful drugs.

II. Inability to Trust People: People who have managed to escape the brainwashing cycle (successful or otherwise) appear to withdraw into themselves, and are unable to trust anyone they encounter after their experience, whether a stranger or someone they adore with all their hearts.

III. Everything is a Test: After a brainwashing phase, a lot of life tends to lose its thrill. The victim no longer takes part in hobbies that they once loved; they completely lose motivation and hope for the future. Any time they are given a chance to join in or asked to be involved in an assignment, they pull apart and examine all the details before deciding whether or not it is something they want to take part in.

Chapter 14: Learn How To Use Manipulation To Your Advantage

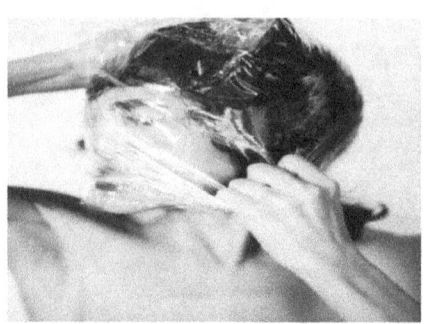

A successful manipulator must have tactics at hand that will help them succeed at persuading people to achieve their own end goal. Although there are extreme theories that describe what a successful manipulator should be,

Simon says that the manipulator will require to:

Hide their aggressive behaviors and intentions from the person or people they want to manipulate.

Determine the weaknesses of their intended subject or victims to identify the tactics that will help achieve their goals.

Develop some degree of brutality not to handle any doubts that arise because of harming the subjects if it arrives. This harm can either be emotional or physical.

The motivating feature in manipulative interaction

Right now, you are aware that a significant characteristic of manipulative interaction is the realization that "deliberate action" is the right choice for him in a particular situation. The manipulator's ability to change the critical capacity to destroy the judgment may interfere with the target's awareness. Still, it doesn't result in a change of direction.

It means that blurring and clouding affecting the critical capacity does not stimulate the "desirable" track. A strong incentive is needed to ensure that deliberate action is the first in the target's scale of choice. To realize this effect, the manipulator requires creating a link between the intentional act and the achievement of a powerful wish.

For the most part, the manipulator awakens a strong force in the subject's mind. He builds the notion that his plan will succeed if the target sticks to the manipulator's instructions. The motivating factor in manipulative interaction shows a gap between the manipulator and the target. The target is trying to realize a powerful wish while the manipulator encourages him to use incentives that create a false impression.

Manipulation as a motivating behavior

Manipulation is a motivating action. It is an effort by a person to make their colleague behave in a certain way and for a specific purpose. The decision to manipulate and not apply a direct technique shows that the interaction participants have opposing stands. Robert Godin, in his report Manipulatory Politics, lists and criticizes a neo-Marxist view that describes the contradiction results from various interests. Manipulation works against the interest of those being manipulated. From this perspective, it is implicit that any encouraging action applied for the target's advantage could never be part of the manipulation. It means the neo-Marxist view excludes the entire side of partially positive manipulations concentrating on progressing the target's interests. Godin, who attempts to suggest an enhanced approach to the study of manipulative behavior, considers that the contradiction is facilitated by various wills and not virtually by contradicting interests, that is, "One person—causing the other to act contrary to his putative will."

Godin's definition, which concentrates on contradictory wills, considers that the target's will, or at least his putative will, is always open to the manipulator. Usually enough, human beings like to speak in a different and contradictory voice simultaneously, making it difficult to understand what they want.

Consider this, the rich housewife who keeps complaining that the maintenance task causes her to feel miserable, frustrated, and unhappy, but she refuses to employ someone to help her. How could we forget to talk about the miserable Don Juan, who wants to get married, but continually has love affairs only with married women? And perhaps there is a tragic example of the excellent musician who dedicated most of her life to learning opera's art. She keeps avoiding other beautiful opportunities to audition in front of famous conductors who could assist her in expanding her professional career.

These three tragic heroes, the miserable housewives, frustrated Don Juan. The desperate musician is great examples that ambiguity regarding one's intention will originate from the fact that he is confused and cannot decide. Ironically, manipulative interference can help the toddler understand his will and arrive at a decision. Indeed, so many psychotherapy and education techniques are designed to support a confused person to discover his purpose and choose what to do with it.

Godin's definition also appears problematic in scenarios where the manipulator and the target tend to share the same objectives. In those particular associations, the motivation to apply a manipulative approach can be pushed by different purposes on opportunities to complete the will, such as when the target needs to satisfy his will and realize his goals.

We can now look at Goodin's definition, like an indirect move that is executed out of fear that a direct approach will face opposition.

But this broad preliminary definition demands a lot of care. In some cases, the decision to change depends wholly on efficiency, where the manipulator tries to avoid lengthy explanations and save time and effort. An extreme case is a leader who predicts a political crisis that demands a fast response. He assumes that describing his friends' situation is a waste of time and decides to manipulate them.

Manipulation builds a free choice illusion

Manipulation is changing the target to behave so that, under normal conditions, he resisted.

However, most manipulative approaches are to cause the target to behave in a manner that is not in line with his intentions, interests, and motivations.

This property of manipulative behavior looks paradoxical. On the flipside, causing someone to act contrary to the priorities and preferences shows that manipulation has compelling aspects. On the other hand, the phrase manipulation itself, which is related to an elusive phenomenon like "maneuvering," indicates that the target contains some judgment and consideration while he works. This tension can be corrected by including "illusory free choice" in the description of manipulative interaction.

Overall, the complex manipulator attempts to interfere, intrude, and influence the target's decision-making process by sending the impression that he selects the actions freely and independently. To accomplish this impact, the manipulator tries to make the target see the "intentional action" as the best available choice in the present situation. The practical definition is that the target, subject to a hidden effect, believes that his intentions are made independently and freely.

Hiding vital information to attain the desired decision demonstrates the concept of "illusory free choice" in a manipulative interaction. The target, who knows that he selects the best available option freely and independently, is prone to invisible interference in critical thinking and judgment.

Unfortunately, it is not hard to imagine opposite scenarios where an individual is convinced that he is on the right track, making the best decision, and not ready to consider other choices. Ironically, assisting him in understanding the value of other possibilities demands applying the unconventional methods of influence that specific manipulative strategies can deliver.

In the most challenging situations, the individual is held up in a narrow conception of reality that is not ready to assess critically. There are various classic examples: the ambiguous young gentleman who is prepared to become a great musician although he doesn't have any sense of rhythm; the courageous general who doesn't want to accept the fact that the enemy is going to attack, the diligent manufacturer who spends most of his money, effort, and time improving the quality of goods that are not in demand.

Instances of tragic entrenchment are costly because they limit the world perception of the trapped individual, destroy his adaptation to the continually changing cases of reality, and cause him and his environment a lot of misery and suffering. The relevant point is that a complex manipulative process can sometimes be the only hope in this case. An indirect approach can convince the entrenched target to think twice about the validity of his biased stand.

In the following case, the manipulator can assist the entrenched target to look for other alternatives that he was not even ready to acknowledge. Paradoxically, in the initial stand, the target was aware that he was selecting the best available choice. At the same time, it is the manipulative interference that allowed him to make a real choice.

This strategy can be described as "liberation by manipulation." Briefly, this approach requires methods of influence in psychotherapy and education to develop the impression that the target is doing the change by himself. He is not supposed to realize that someone else is triggering the situation and assisting him in identifying the path to change and improvement.

Hide Manipulation from the target

Motivating, by applying manipulative approaches, intends to restrict any possibility of the target objecting to the manipulator's moves. The manipulator tries to prevent the target from considering specific operational options, or the manipulator attempts to cause the target to factor possible actions that he refuses to assess. The manipulator tries to realize the motivating effect smoothly and elegantly. He wishes to build the impression that the target is selecting his actions freely and independently.

We can accomplish this effect because the process of manipulative interaction, the manipulator's field of vision, is broader than the target. In other words, the manipulator tends to know a lot than the target. It means the manipulator can use the point of view of the target without the target being aware.

However, the target's ability to learn about the manipulator's real intention provides him with the chance to consider other options apart from the goal of the manipulator.

The manipulator wants to prevent; otherwise, she would not move forward with the manipulation. The practical meaning is that the purpose has been exposed, and the target can choose whether to surrender or refuse to cooperate based on the manipulator's instructions. So, it's not a matter of "illusory free choice" but real free choice. For that reason, the manipulative act fails or does not exist.

Based on the characterization, statements such as "you are manipulating me" are self-contradictions. It is not possible to become a victim of manipulation and, at the same time, be aware of it. Additionally, this confronting method was likely applied to change roles in the interaction. One way is that by leveling the accusation, you are trying to discover your hidden intentions.

Another way is to consider the statement "you are manipulating me" as an indirect message. In this case, "I am surrendering, but you have to know that you owe me." In a situation where the manipulator fails to see it, he gets exposed to the possibility of future pressure without knowing it. The manipulator's focus of vision is smaller than the target's, and the practical meaning is that the initial manipulator fell into his trap and became a victim of manipulation.

Manipulation changes the critical capacity

Critical capacity is a relevant mechanism that allows us to choose our actions based on our preferences and priorities. It is supposed to work like a dedicated guard whose responsibility is to maintain our decisions and behavior consistent with our self-interest and world perspective.

An encouraging action meant to direct a person to behave in contradiction to his choices without realizing the distortion must interfere or avoid the inspection procedure. The manipulative activity aims to affect the target's critical capacity. Two strategies are intended to achieve this:

The first one is obvious. The manipulator applies morally questionable approaches during the interaction to prevent any likely objection to the target's moves. However, changing critical capacity can be applied to the advantage of the manipulator, and it could be used to enhance the target's stand.

The first example markets Erich Fromm's description of manipulative techniques applied by modern advertising to counteract critical judgment and encourage the selling of useless or irrelevant goods. According to Fromm's definition, a vast sector of contemporary advertising does not appeal to reason but emotion.

The second example is derived from the field of psychotherapy. Milton Erickson's confusing style is meant to confuse the target. The concept is to destroy the target's critical capacity and make him work in a direction different from his intentions and priorities.

Overall, Erickson created and used the confusion technique for hypnosis. He and colleagues applied the same process in psychotherapy to confuse patients for a relevant change. The confusion decreases the patient's critical judgment and destroys his everyday resistance to changing traditional habits that make him suffer. By reducing the target's critical awareness, Erickson expected to pave ways to discover new methods.

The second approach is meant to enhance and improve the target's critical capacity. But we should not forget that changing essential ability is also a manipulative process. The final result of manipulation is to make the target behave to refuse otherwise. We have a fundamental reason to doubt that the sophisticated manipulator only wants to develop the impression of assisting the target in developing and explaining his critical capacity. The real intention is quite different.

The example involves a manipulative workshop for creating critical capacity. A matchmaker is selected to choose a perfect bride for a young Jew. The young man who commits most of his time to study the bible has never dated a lady in his lifetime. As a great student, he learns from his mentor that the bride's value is determined based on her family's status. "The secret to a great marriage is that the bride comes from a good family," says the matchmaker.

Armed with this knowledge, our young hero goes for the first date to meet an unattractive, spoiled lady whose wealthy father "accidentally" paid the matchmaker a lot of money.

Funny stories involving manipulative strategies in traditional societies resemble rigid approaches to sales promotion in modern times. Most of the time, we need to purchase a device whose functions we don't understand, and we don't know how to compare several products. We step into the shop, and an elegant salesman is ready to assist. Tiny cases involve those where the manipulator has an excellent estimation of the target's preference. However, the potential to change critical capacity does not require this awareness. For instance, it can be sufficient to apply psychological knowledge and mathematical expertise to trigger a person's decision. A popular technique is to develop a decision-making problem that would damage any possible objection to the manipulator's desired result. An individual's choice can be reversed by defining a particular choice problem separately. If delivered as a choice between gains, one will probably go for the less risky option. But if it is offered as a choice between losses, one will go for the more dangerous option.

In general, the manipulator affects the target's decision by believing that he decides the best available option in a particular case. The target's understanding or misunderstanding of the situation shows that his critical capacity is paralyzed. In the following case, the manipulator can realize this effect through rational arguments, temptation, etc. The crucial point here is that manipulative behavior, as good as it may be, focuses on diminishing the target's potential to judge the manipulator's moves critically.

Conclusion

Now that you can recognize who the manipulators may be in your life (or whether you've been guilty of using these techniques as well), identify signs of being manipulated, and learn how to handle them, you can better evaluate the relationships around you to make the educated choices you need in your own life. Through a more realistic view of life, you may share your thoughts, opinions, and wishes without feeling guilty, realizing that they are indeed your own.

You can detect and understand persuasion and manipulation signals by evaluating and examining your relationships' contact signs. When that is evident, you will exercise your right to be treated with dignity. In a contact exchange, you regain the power and right to be equal individuals to yourself. In a relationship with an equal balance of control, you can say 'no' without feeling guilty. You can set your goals to build a better life or world for yourself and others you care for.

The ability to interpret people's body language and see beyond misleading phrases stops you from being extorted or abused unknowingly. You are more open to opportunities around you and less likely to be affected by others' purpose and motivated by it. But being able to identify those tactics means that you too can manipulate these tricks. Be sure to consult with your moral compass and be always mindful of treating each person as an equal citizen, worthy of the right to be treated and free to choose.

The principle of Dark Psychology assumes you're ignorant of past devious actions or just do not care. Here's an opportunity to change the trajectory of yours and start anew. Whatever predatory actions you've engaged in, criminal and sociopathic, there's usually a decision to cease, desist, and part from the abyss of getting sociopathic.

The head's capability might be said to be very vast, and this might be said that the individuals that see how the mind of their functions might tend to get much more out of life. Additionally, learning how you can take control of the mind of yours might enable you to be in charge of the points that occur in daily life. Thus, rather than allowing life to come about for you, you can decide what goes on in the life of yours. The survivalist mentality is the norm of ours. This what society tries to do is manage the wild beast in every man by teaching them out of an early age to obey the laws, morals, and rules of the controlling team, typically the rich, who dominate our institutions and governments.

www.ingramcontent.com/pod-product-compliance
Lightning Source LLC
Chambersburg PA
CBHW071433070526
44578CB00001B/88